The Curious Learner

Help Your Child Develop Academic and Creative Skills

The Successful Learner Series

Series editor,
Carl B. Smith, Ph.D.

Also in this series:

The Confident Learner:
Help Your Child Succeed in School

The Curious Learner

Help Your Child Develop Academic and Creative Skills

Marjorie R. Simic • Melinda McClain
Michael Shermis

GRAYSON BERNARD
P U B L I S H E R S

Family Literacy
Center

Cover art and illustrations by Dave Coverly
Book design by Kathleen McConahay and
    Addie Seabarkrob
Cover layout by Addie Seabarkrob

Library of Congress Cataloging-in-Publication Data

Simic, Marjorie R. (Marjorie Rose), 1951–
    The curious learner: help you child develop academic
and creative skills / Marjorie R. Simic, Melinda mcClain,
Michael Shermis.

        p. cm. -- (The Successful learner series)
    Includes bibliographical references (p.) and index.
    ISBN 0–9628556–8–5

    1. Education, Elementary--United States--Parent
participation. 2. Education, Preschool--United States--
Parent participation. 3. Creative ability. I. McClain,
Melinda, 1958–   . II. Shermis. Michael, 1959–   .
III. Title. IV. Series.

    LB1048.5.S56 1992   649'.68--dc20   92–27708

Grayson Bernard Publishers
223 S. Pete Ellis Drive, Suite 12
P.O. Box 5247
Bloomington, Indiana 47407

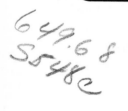

About the Authors

Marjorie R. Simic is a former Chapter I teacher and coordinator. She is currently a writer and program evaluator for the Family Literacy Center at Indiana University where she is completing her Ed.S. in Language Education. She has published and made numerous presentations on parent involvement in education.

Melinda McClain is the editorial assistant for the *Parents and Children Together* audio magazine published by the Family Literacy Center and serves as User Services Specialist for the *Parents Sharing Books* program.

Michael Shermis is assistant director of the Family Literacy Center and serves as editor of *Parents and Children Together*, a monthly audio magazine. He also coordinates the *Parents Sharing Books* program, a training program for leaders who teach parents to share books with their children.

Contents

Acknowledgments   ix

A Note to Parents   xi

Chapter 1:
The Curious Learner   1

Chapter 2:
Learning Science at Home   19

Chapter 3:
Learning Math at Home   37

Chapter 4:
Making History Come Alive   55

Chapter 5:
Using the Library   75

Contents

Chapter 6:
Making Writing Meaningful   93

Chapter 7:
Appreciating Poetry   109

Chapter 8:
Enjoying Art all around Us   127

Chapter 9:
**Creative Expression through Music
and Dance**   141

Index   155

Acknowledgments

Thanks, once again, to the staff at Grayson Bernard for their help. Susan Yerolemou has been enjoyable to work with, Kathleen McConahay has done a fine job with the desktop publishing, and Gene Reade has been helpful with the first chapter and index. Several people from the staff at the Family Literacy Center need to be mentioned for their help, including Susan Moke (who helped significantly with one chapter), Becky Stiles, Sonja Rasmussen, and Ellie Macfarlane for their proofreading; Kay White for her typing; and Rhonda Critchlow, Jennifer Rendell, and Jamillah Muhammad for other numerous tasks. As always, our artist, Dave Coverly, has provided us with cartoons that illustrate our points well and add that twist of humor to our words. And, of course, thanks to Carl Smith for giving us so many opportunities to change families' lives.

Marge Simic thanks the children with whom she has had the privilege to work. When they succeed, only then do we know that parents and teachers together did their job.

Melinda McClain thanks the Lilly Endowment for their support and gifts that provide many children with the opportunity to become life-long learners.

Michael Shermis thanks Laura Dorsey and Jeannette Olson for all of the advice and friendship they have offered the last few years. They have contributed greatly to his success in numerous ways.

A Note to Parents

There are numerous questions your children will ask you during their years in school. Although this book doesn't contain answers to particular questions they are asking, it does direct you to the many sources that will help you deal with their questions. It also provides you with practical ideas and activities that will prompt you and your child to remain curious learners. Chapters two through four deal with the important subjects of science, math, and history; the fifth reminds you of ways to use the library. The remaining chapters describe your role in the important arts of self-expression.

The many activities in every chapter in this book will help your children find ways to apply what they know and discover their personal interests and abilities. There are activities for fun and learning, for exploring science and history, for using the library, for appreciating poetry, and for self-expression through music, dance, and the arts.

Each chapter also has lists of books: books for you to read to find out more about the topic, and books for you to share with your children. These book lists are divided into age categories: 4–6, 6–8, 8–10.

If you are the kind of person who likes to listen rather than read, these topics are on audio cassettes. Each audio cassette also contains read-along stories which you and your children can listen to together. Information about ordering these audio cassettes can be found at the back of this book.

Now, begin the journey that you and your children can take towards helping them become curious learners and well-rounded individuals who succeed in school and in life.

The Curious Learner

Why is the moon white? How many stars are there in the sky? Were there dinosaurs here when Grandpa was a boy? Who invented spaghetti?

Questions, questions, questions—young children often sound like bundles of questions. All of us parents go through the stage where our children drive us crazy with questions. They have come to realize the power of words like *who, why, how, what.* Their curiosity seems insatiable. And they have discovered a new way to learn—by asking questions.

All of us can take a cue from our young children. We would all learn more if we turned up the heat on our curiosity. Instead of discouraging questions (because they drive us crazy) we should promote them and add questions of our own. "I don't know why the moon looks white. Let's look in the encyclopedia. I wonder, too, why we see the whole moon sometimes and other times we only see part of the moon. If the encyclopedia doesn't answer our questions, we can ask our neighbor, Mrs. Swander. She teaches science at the middle school."

That kind of conversation shows your child that you both are curious people; you both have unanswered questions. Indirectly you are praising your child and you are stimulating your own curiosity at the same time. If you are going to continue to learn, you must remain curious. If you want your child to learn, you must stimulate his or her curiosity, too. That attitude of curiosity means just as much during the school years as it does during the preschool years when we sometimes feel that the only thing that comes from our children's mouths is questions.

In this book we show you how to develop this invaluable curiosity toward specific school subjects and toward creative expressions that your children perform in school. In a companion book called *The Confident Learner*, we stressed this important point:

The child who succeeds is one who has a sense of direction and feels reasonably secure in tackling the learning problems of school and life. In this book we give you specific ways that you can expand the work your child does in school subjects by applying them in the home and to the daily activities that your family shares. By reinforcing your child's school work in the home, you give him a sense of direction and security. Your child will have both curiosity and confidence when dealing with all areas of learning.

Studies of successful children reveal parents who are actively helping their children throughout their school years. We know, for instance, that when parents show an interest in school learning by asking questions, children perk up and achieve higher grades in those subjects. And there is a clear trend for the future. Those people who have knowledge, are well-schooled, and are willing to learn constantly will far outdistance their co-workers in holding satisfactory jobs and in living comfortable lives. The people who fit that description usually come from homes where parents showed an energetic interest in school subjects and regularly encouraged their children to ask questions and to express themselves creatively.

To help you succeed in your important role of parent, there are two common themes in each chapter of *The Curious Learner*. The first is an emphasis on showing you how to apply school subject knowledge to everyday activities. The second is the idea that knowledge from various subjects can be woven together so that they complement one another. The novels we read, for example, may help us understand a period in history. Searching for those connections is the hallmark of the curious learner.

Paying Attention to the Obvious

How do subjects such as science and history concern you as a parent? Don't your children study them in school? Isn't that sufficient? Not if you want your child to be an active learner. There are many things you can do to show your child how important these subjects are and how much they are used all the time.

We can hardly go through a single day without encountering some aspect of science, math, and history. Many of these situations are so simple and commonplace that we hardly notice them:

Science:
"Did you cover up the rose bushes? The temperature is supposed to drop below freezing tonight."

"That water will never boil unless you turn the heat up higher."

"I hope the pipes don't burst. It's supposed to be very cold tonight."

In each of these examples we are concerned with the effect of high or low temperatures on familiar objects: rose bushes, a pan of water, or pipes.

Math:

"How much more lumber will we need? This fence is ten and a half feet long, but I've only got one six-foot board."

"I don't think we'll get there on time. We've got 50 miles to go. In this traffic we'll never make it in an hour."

"I have only two quarters and a dime. Can you lend me enough money to buy this notebook for $1.29?"

Here we are concerned with measurement: of length, of time, and of quantity.

History:

"When did Grandpa Elvis say he would get back from Albuquerque? I want to call him as soon as he returns."

"Isn't this amazing? Babe Ruth hit 714 home runs in his career and batted .342 for a lifetime average! No wonder people think he was a great player!"

"Did you know that Leonardo da Vinci created a design for a type of helicopter *almost 500 years ago*?

All of these examples cause us to look back and to remember something in the past. The first question has immediate importance; it focuses on something that happened recently (Grandpa's trip to Albuquerque) in order to help us determine what we will do next. The other two questions help us to understand things we do today (playing baseball, flying) by making us aware of how they developed in the more distant past.

5

You can help your child see that she has just used her knowledge of science to decide what to do about rose bushes in cold weather, or that he has used his knowledge of math to figure out how much more money he will need for the notebook. Even very young children can come to realize that they are *applying school knowledge* when they deal with everyday situations such as these.

Discovering How the Pieces Fit Together

Once you begin to think about the possibilities, you come to realize that many topics are likely to involve an understanding of science, math, and history to varying degrees. As you and your children begin to see how this works, you will become more and more interested in finding ways to approach a subject or a task from several different angles.

Consider a relatively simple operation, such as baking a cake (from scratch, not from a box). The recipe has a history: It was developed and tried by someone in the past and was found to be successful. How many

cups or teaspoons or tablespoons of each ingredient are required? We must use mathematics to figure quantities. What happens if we leave out an ingredient or cook the batter for too short or too long a time or at the wrong temperature? These questions involve chemistry (the interaction of ingredients) and physics (the effects of heat).

What are some other everyday experiences that can challenge your child to find connecting links? Take a look at the following examples. (The possibilities are endless.)

Taking a trip by car. When were automobiles first developed? Who made the first automobiles that actually ran? How did these older cars work? How do modern cars differ from these older ones? What happens when the fuel is ignited in the engine? How can we figure the distance we have to travel and the time it will take to cover that distance? Which audiotapes shall we take with us?

Going to a movie. How did movies first develop? Who were some of the people involved in the early days? How did movies change from "silents" to "talkies?" How does film manage to record an image? How does a camera work? What were some earlier types of cameras? How does the speed of the film and the amount of light affect the final product? What happens when a film is recorded at one speed but then played back at a different speed? How is music used to give movies more impact?

Having lunch. Why do we think there must be three meals per day? Do people in other cultures follow other customs for meals? What happens to various kinds of food when they are cooked for different periods of time or in different ways (baking, broiling, frying, etc.)? How does the body burn calories? How many calories are needed to run a mile or to play basketball for a half hour (or to eat lunch)?

Visualizing the Pyramid

Now consider a subject that few of us have encountered at first hand: the great pyramids of Egypt. As children move through the early grades, they usually read about these huge stone monuments, or they see pictures of them in books or in movies and on TV. What better example of a topic that involves all the subjects we have been talking about?

First of all, the pyramids are certainly of great historical importance. In them we see some of the things that were accomplished during the flowering of ancient Egyptian civilization many thousands of years ago. As we read about the pyramids, we want to know when they were built and what they were used for. What was going on in other early civilizations at the same time? Have you seen pictures of the ornate gold objects that were placed in the tombs of the pharaohs? Are there any pyramids anywhere else closer to home? (Yes: Mexico.) Can you find a pyramid used as a symbol on a well-known piece of paper that most of us see every day? (Try the dollar bill.)

Mathematics obviously enters the picture as well. What is the shape of the *pyramid*? What would it look like from the side? Can you think of any other examples of pyramid structures? Why was this a good shape for these monuments? How would *you* build a pyramid of individual blocks of stone or wood?

In terms of science, children can first learn about the materials used to build these gigantic structures. Why were limestone blocks used? Were they readily available? Other early civilizations, such as those of Greece and Rome, constructed bridges and aqueducts, statues and buildings from other stones, especially marble and granite. Why are these stones good for construction? These are all questions that show the relationship between history and science. Furthermore, the study of physics can help us understand more about the pyramids. How were those enormous blocks moved over long distances? How were they lifted several hundred feet from the ground? The young child does not need to know that these problems involve physics: It is enough to know that there are logical ways to find the answers.

Using What We Already Know

There is no question that knowledge of science, math, and history can help us with everyday problems or projects such as baking a cake or mending a fence or tending to plants. You can help your children understand that school work applies to things they do in their own lives. Science and math show us that problems can be solved if we apply our knowledge in a logical way. History shows us *how* something developed over time and *why* it is the way it is today. All of these subjects help to broaden our perspective, to see a given subject or event as part of a larger framework. These are among the most important lessons to be learned in any area of study.

In the chapter on science, we stress the importance of the child's *curiosity* (How does the spider build a web?) and the importance of *play* (What happens if we turn this upside down?). These are characteristics we observe in the development of younger children in particular. As they grow older, children discover that trial-and-error experiments can lead to more logical approaches and can help them develop *flexible thinking* (What happens if we change something? If that

didn't work, maybe this will). With practice, children learn how to avoid becoming locked into a single way of looking at things. All of these activities challenge thought and show children that there are often several ways to approach a problem. Furthermore, all of these experiments can be made with actual objects and with problems that arise in everyday life.

With mathematics, the child learns to develop solutions that rely on computation rather than on trial and error. We don't have to cut ten different lengths of wood or try various combinations in order to fix something: We can measure and use numbers to plan our approach on paper. Like science, mathematics also helps children learn that there may be more than one way to deal with a problem, but it does even more. It shows them how to take a logical approach and to make reasonable estimates that can guide their thinking. All they need is a few good questions.

Space flight interests many children. Of course this involves science and math of the highest order, but it can be understood more fully if we look at history as well. The Space Shuttle is often in the news. When did the first shuttle flight take place? What other kinds of space flight preceded it? When did astronauts first go to the moon? When did the first spacecraft go into orbit? How did people think about flight in earlier centuries, even before it was technically possible? By viewing space flight in a broader context, children can come to appreciate just how remarkable an achievement it is.

As children's curiosity leads them to explore these subjects more extensively, they will want to broaden their knowledge by drawing on the resources of libraries. Books can be supplemented by the wealth of material available on audio and video recordings. Children can not only read historical accounts of the first trip to the moon; they can go back to newspapers and magazines published at the time of the landing, or they can see it on video recording. As they explore the library, children discover that they can hear recordings of the speeches of President Kennedy or President Roosevelt, and they can see programs showing how bridges or buildings were constructed. All of these resources can do much to satisfy the curiosity of children and to motivate them to expand their knowledge in areas that interest them.

Nurturing the Arts of Self-Expression

There is no question that subjects such as science, math, and history are important areas which form the core of much school work. However, young children need to be able to develop all of their potential for expression, and the arts play a vitally important role in this development. Music, dance, and drawing help children understand their heritage and their culture.

Much of our self-expression is done through writing. The ability to write clearly is just as important as the ability to think clearly. In fact, the two can hardly be separated. Don't overlook the fact that good writing is as important to the child's feeling of self-worth as it is to school work.

Look at the following composition, written by a fifth-grader. It is a remarkable example of all the things we have been talking about.

The Near Disaster

It was a dark, freezing cold night. The wind was blowing fiercely around my small hut. My name is Anna. I came over with the first shipload of Puritans. There came a knock at the door. I got

up from my rocker to answer it. I opened the door and a blast of icy wind came rushing in. In the doorway stood Governor Bradford. He explained why he had come. "I just wanted to make sure you were all right, Anna. It's a bad storm out there, you know."

"Oh yes, Governor. I'm quite fine. Would you like to stay for some coffee?"

"Thank you, I think I will."

We talked awhile until he said, "Well, I must be going. I have to make sure everyone else is all right. Thank you very much for the coffee."

"Oh, you're quite welcome, Governor Bradford."

"Are you sure you'll be all right, Anna?"

"Oh yes, I'm sure I'll be quite all right." But that was not the truth. The truth was that I was very scared. What if the hut collapsed? What if I were killed? I knew there was a very slim chance of this happening, but I was still scared.

The next morning, the sun was shining brightly and birds were singing. I got up, dressed, and hurried outside. My goodness! The village was a shambles. Everyone was soon working, trying to salvage some of the damage. Some houses collapsed, and the church was a wreck. Everybody was rushing about, shouting and taking orders. I joined in.

In three weeks, we had most of the damage fixed. Our new church was almost done and most of the homes that had been damaged were fixed.

I went back to my comfortable little hut and sat down. While I rested I thought, "We were lucky to have been able to save most of our village. We might not have been able to do it at all! I was glad our town was back to normal."

The few misspelled words (and there were only four) have been corrected here. Other details can be refined with time. The important thing is that this student has written a very interesting story, one that not only involves a dramatic event but also shows how people reacted to that event. She has presented a clear narrative to the reader, complete with dialogue and remarkably sophisticated language and sentence structure for a fifth-grader. Even more significantly, she has drawn upon her knowledge of history *to place herself as a character in a story set in the early seventeenth century.*

This kind of writing brings together several positive features: clear sentence structure and good use of language; an interesting story that involves real people; a personal involvement in the drama; and a historical setting which shows that the student has been affected by her study of the early colonial period in

America. Her study of this historical period has become an important part of her own experience; it is not merely an abstract "school subject" that was learned because it was required.

Good, clear writing can certainly serve the cause of self-expression. By placing herself in the story, this girl has intensified the feelings of fear as the storm raged and of relief when it had passed. Younger children often express their own feelings and experience in stories or in poems, but it is unusual for a student in the early grades to be able to carry this into a situation that she did not experience at first hand. A story such as this shows just how much students can accomplish when they discover that everything they learn and everything they do can be interwoven to form an effective expression of ideas.

The Arts Connection

Even though writing is the most common form of self-expression, music, dance, and visual arts should be promoted, too. Those art forms open doors to many learners who do not feel comfortable writing stories and explanations. Children can express their feelings and their ideas through motion, through song, and through pictures, as well as through words. We assume that your school offers these artistic forms of learning, and we encourage you to extend them at home. Your questions and your interest in the performing and the visual arts give them legitimacy for your children. Your enthusiasm for artistic creativity will encourage your children not only to study the arts in school, but also to use them as a means of self-expression.

Are the arts truly beneficial to your children? you may wonder. Many studies show that students who have four or more years of music and art succeed better in academic tasks than those who have invested less time. The College Entrance Examination Board, for example, found that those who had more experience in music and art scored higher on their SAT tests than those who had less experience. And a University of California study indicates that those with more experience in the arts show greater improvement in reading, writing, speaking, social studies, science and math.

In fact, having arts in the curriculum has risen to such importance that at least two states have been sued when they failed to provide regular funds for school arts. Lawsuits against the states of Kentucky and Louisiana have been initiated by concerned citizens. They feel that children learn significant aspects of their heritage and their culture through the arts. If are deprived of regular exposure to the arts and to the benefits of artistic expression, so the suits argue, then they do not receive equal opportunities in learning through their most effective means.

It may interest you to know that only nine states mandate an arts curriculum for high school students. Yet the U.S. Department of Labor issued a report urging schools to teach for the workplace of the future. The skills they called for—working in teams, creative thinking, imagination, and invention—are the same skills fostered by arts education.

All the arts are important to children, especially in the early years. Some children will have special aptitudes for art or music or dance or writing; these innate talents can be nurtured as part of the child's growth and development. However, even if children do not exhibit talents in a particular art, they can certainly learn to *appreciate* all of them. Encourage your children to enhance their appreciation by expressing

themselves in words or music or painting or dance. Praise their efforts to use these means of self-expression, no matter what the artistic impression.

As a parent, you can help your child see that school subjects are important and that they do apply to everyday life. You can also do much to support your child's efforts toward self-expression, regardless of the forms this may take. If your child is a curious, well-rounded learner—one who is interested and willing to explore all areas of learning—he or she will have great chances for success in school and in life. Draw upon the ideas in this book to build upon the curiosity, the imagination, and the inventiveness that your child already possesses.

Learning Science at Home

When you watch a spider construct a web and marvel at the design or its strength in holding other insects, you are engaging in science. When you jack up a car to change a tire, you are using a lever to lift an object too heavy to lift with your own strength. That's science. When you spray an extra strong cleaner on a stubborn dirt spot and see that spot dissolve, you are watching science. The list of your daily activities that involve you in science is quite long.

Science is nothing more than the study of the physical and natural world in which we live. Anytime, therefore, that you ask a question about nature or try to figure out how something works, you are being a scientist; you are engaging in science. The study of science in school helps students understand the facts and the principles that make some part of our world work.

At home with your child, you can make science easier and more valuable by asking questions and encouraging your child to ask questions about the world around him. That's what scientists do. In fact, they think that asking questions to seek information or to solve a problem is so important that they give that activity a special name. They call it "inquiry", that is, the orderly search for knowledge by asking questions and collecting information.

Science may sound like heavy business, with all that orderly questioning and searching going on, but for children it is just natural. One of the best ways to enable them to solve science problems as a matter of fact, is through play. Einstein said that that is what he did: he often arrived at a logical answer through a kind of "vague play," that is, he played "what if" games in his mind to explore new ideas. Probably most of us learn a lot about the world around us through "vague play."

We play with potted plants by shifting them in the sunlight, by giving them more or less water, and even by talking to them to help them grow. Through that kind of play we learn how best to grow certain plants in our house, in our yards and in our environment. Simply by talking about what we are doing with plants or laundry soaps or the tools we use for home repairs, we help our children develop inquiring minds.

We can't emphasize enough the value of play in making science interesting. With young children, building blocks are excellent science play. Whether using old fashioned wooden blocks or plastic ones that snap together, children learn about balance, symmetry, and other principles of construction by simply playing with building blocks. Later, when they are able to use tools safely, children can learn some basic physical principles by nailing pieces of wood together, trying to construct a toy or a birdhouse, or repairing something that is broken. Play is a non-threatening way to face life and to solve some of the physical or chemical problems in our lives. The great Swiss psychologist Jean Piaget viewed play as an essential learning process because it's a way for children to feel and think, and it is a way to come into contact with failure and success while working with other people and with nature.

Play helps develop flexible thinking and motivation—important ingredients in scientific problem solving. So when you explore the world with your child, first try to produce large numbers of ideas. In a make-believe world, for example, you can try all kinds of solutions. Do you remember the fairy tale about Rapunzel who had hair so long that the handsome prince could climb into her prison tower by making a rope ladder from her hair? How else might he have gotten up there? More questions provide more opportunities for the thinker to solve problems.

A flexible thinker is willing to try different strategies for solving a problem. One of the reasons that certain toys are so valuable is that they promote flexibility. Studies have shown that children who have played with blocks, constructive toys, and puzzles are more willing to search for a variety of solutions than children whose experiences have been mostly with structured play and who therefore are more likely to use a rigid single strategy to solve a problem.

How about motivation to learn science? As with any learning, science learning depends on motivation. One of the characteristics of learning through play is that play usually provides its own built-in motivation. As they play a situation to its conclusion, children can be imaginative, self-directed, and spontaneous, all characteristics of children's play.

Since science learning and problem solving are closely linked, here are some guidelines that will help you work with your child to promote real-world problem-solving:

❖ Encourage your child to play with concrete objects such as blocks, boxes, string, rope, and stacking objects.

❖ Ask questions out loud and try to figure out the answers with your child. You may be surprised by her fresh solutions.

❖ Show interest by asking your child about school experiments and then try to relate them to things that happen at home—following recipes, boiling water, or constructing models. Allow time for your child to ask questions and don't be afraid to learn together.

❖ Let problem-solving skills develop gradually. Don't push. They need time to take shape.

❖ Take family field trips to the zoo, science museum, aquarium, and library regularly.

❖ Give science-focused books or magazine subscriptions as birthday and holiday presents.

❖ Watch a science-related television show with your child once a week, and talk about it.

❖ Try experiments at home; for example, float a drinking straw in plain water, and then in salt water. Because of the density of salt water, objects that sink in plain water will float in salt water. Or give your child a magnet and let him see if he can determine what sticks to the magnet and what does not.

Opportunities for making science interesting and real are everywhere. All we have to do is to ask standard science questions, like:

What is it?
How does it work?
How can I change it?

These will lead to more specific questions, such as:

What makes the body work?
What makes the world work?
How do the stars and planets stay on course?

But don't make science at home a heavy or serious experience. Relax and enjoy answering questions with your child. Learn to be a scientist right along with your child. That means ask, explore, play with ideas, and try to make sense of the world around you. When things don't work out, laugh and start the process all over again. If you can laugh at the trial-and-error play of being a scientist, so will your child. Then he will tackle school science with the same friendly attitude.

Questions about Science

❖ **I would like to help my children see the importance of studying science in school. How can I do science at home with my children that will encourage this?**

As a parent, you can do a lot to help your children learn science. Children are scientists by nature—they have an almost unquenchable curiosity. Encourage your children to be inquisitive, to be investigators, and show them that you are curious also. Here are a few examples:

* Take apart an old toaster, bike, or flashlight so your children can see how it works.

* Use bird and squirrel feeders to attract wildlife to your yard. Explore with your children what they observe—feeding habits and protective behavior.

❖   Plant flower and vegetable gardens. Talk about
    the different types of seeds, seedlings, and
    plants. Observe the growth by charting or record-
    ing weather, precipitation, and plant growth each
    day. Are there relationships between these
    factors?

❖   Make daily observations of the sun and the
    moon. Discuss the changing shape of the moon
    and the position of the sun in the winter and
    summer.

❖   Take a walk. Bring back some seeds and plant
    them.

❖   Plant an herb garden in a window box and use
    the herbs in cooking.

❖   Watch science and nature programs with your
    child on educational television. Ask questions
    together about what you see.

❖ Build models from kits with your child. Discuss construction principles and techniques.

❖ Share your own hobbies. For example, if you are a hiker, biker, or camper, take your children along. Introduce them to animals, trees, plants, and everything the outdoors has to offer.

At Christmastime and for birthdays, buy children's gifts that encourage curiosity, questions, and further explorations. Even very young children will be fascinated by a microscope, a telescope, a magnifying glass, or a compass if they are shown how to use them.

❷ **Chemistry sets and science kits for the home are so expensive. Do you have any affordable alternatives?**

Science at home should be what I refer to as "shoestring science." That means collecting and saving almost everything from string to tinfoil. The key to successful, creative sciencing at home is to adopt the substitution habit. Substitute a peanut butter jar for scientific glassware.

When you need:	Substitute:
flashlight casings	toilet paper rolls
vials	pill bottles
eyedroppers	soda straws
weights	fishing sinkers
containers	coffee and film cans
wheels	skates, bikes, toy cars
mirrors	aluminum foil on cardboard
graduated cylinders	baby bottles/medicine cups
density objects	clay
copper tubing or pipe	iron or aluminum or nails
measuring sticks	paint sticks, licorice, string, straws
wire or string	fishing line
screening	panty hose
stirring rods	tongue depressors, ice cream sticks
scoops or shovels	plastic bleach bottles
culture dishes	plastic margarine tubs
timers	alarm clocks
aquariums	gallon jars
crayfish homes	plastic dish pans

❖ My daughter is having trouble reading her science book from school. She thinks it is difficult and boring. How can I help her develop an interest in reading about science?

By saying the book is difficult and boring, your daughter may be saying one and the same thing. Some people assume something is boring when it is very difficult to read. You might ask her if she is uninterested in the topic. If she says yes, you and her teacher can discuss ways of raising her interests—for example, by engaging in hands-on experiments. If, on the other hand, the book seems too difficult for her to read alone, you can help her tackle that problem by reading with her.

There are many children's books on the market today that focus on science activities and information. You can find books to explain scientific principles in easy-to-read, easy-to-understand format. The library can provide her with numerous information books at her level. Children's encyclopedias such as *Child Craft,* and children's magazines such as *Ranger Rick, ZooBook,* and *World* are all reliable sources that can help your child develop an interest in science.

Children acquire knowledge when they are actively engaged. You may want to help your child do some of the more simple experiments or activities in the science books. Science is much more than just reading about it. Hands-on activities and experiments help your child understand concepts that otherwise may be confusing or unclear.

❖ **My kids are very curious about the physical world, but sometimes their questions drive me crazy. How can I encourage this curiosity in a positive way?**

Children ask questions daily about the world around them. We constantly hear "Why did that happen?" "Why does it work that way?" and "What will happen if...?" It is unrealistic to think that we should be able to answer all their questions. Yet we want our children to ask questions and to be curious. The way we handle questions can influence whether or not children continue to ask about the things around them. At times we need patience, but mostly we need to be honest in saying "I don't know" or "Let's find out together—maybe later, at a more convenient time." Here are a couple of suggestions for handling persistent questions:

❖ Help your children learn to seek answers to their own questions. Instead of giving a verbal answer, suggest an activity that might help your children discover what it is they want to know.

❖ To discover new things, encourage your children to use their own senses, like hearing, listening, tasting, touching, and smelling. Instead of telling your child how many legs a ladybug has, ask your child to take a closer look — "How many legs do you see on that ladybug?"

❖ Ask questions that lead children to answer some of their own questions. Include questions like "I wonder where we could find out about that?" or "How can we solve this problem?"

❖ Show children sources of information, such as encyclopedias, *Child Craft* books, and magazines, that can help them learn more about the things that interest them.

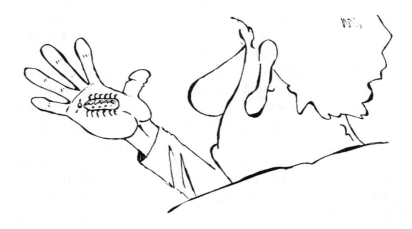

Questioning at home should not be directed solely by the need to train future scientists and engineers (although actually we may be doing this!). Rather, it is an attempt in this complex world to equip children with basic survival skills. It is simply helping them figure things out on their own, to discover how to learn independently.

Activities for Science Learning

Your house is filled with everyday things you can use to help your child understand science. We have listed a few suggestions for some science activities you can do at home, and you don't have to purchase special kits or expensive equipment. Select one for you and your child to do together.

Mini Environment
Pour two teaspoons of water into a plastic bag that will seal securely. Blow air into the bag and seal it. Tape the bag to a window that is in a sunny location. What happens in a few days? (The water cycle occurs in your plastic bag. The water in the bottom represents a body of water, the fog on the sides shows how clouds form, and the drops represent rainfall.)

Pick a Potato
Place two toothpicks in the middle of a sweet potato on opposite sides. Balance the toothpicks on the rim of the jar full of water. Talk with your child about what might happen. Encourage him to watch the potato as it changes during the next few months. He might want to draw pictures of it at different stages, or keep track of the changes in a journal.

Stop Pollution!
Take a walk or a bike ride through your community and look for signs of pollution. Discuss what you see and how the pollution might have occurred. Think of ways your family can help clean up and recycle in your local area.

Bird Fun
Check out a book from your local library about birds that live in your area. Set up a bird feeder outside your window or go to a park that has one. Watch the feeder and when your child spots a bird, help her look it up in the book and read about it.

Books for Parents

Nature for the Very Young: A Handbook of Indoor and Outdoor Activities, by Marcia Bowden. Ideas for parents to help their young children learn about and have fun with nature. Seasons, animals, plants, habitats, and different phenomenons of nature are the basis for the activities in this book.

175 Science Experiments to Amuse and Amaze Your Friends, by Brenda Walpole. Shows experiments parents can do with their children, gives examples of tricks that explain scientific theories, and illustrates things you and your child can make together. Some topics are light, color, sight, balance, air, wind, weather, water, gravity, sound, and motion.

Young Peacemakers Project Book, by Kathleen Fry-Miller and Judith Myers-Walls. Gives guidelines for projects that help care for the environment and promote peace. Topics for the environmental projects are nature, art, outdoor adventure, birds, litterbugs, garbage, clean air and water, energy conservation, and recycling. Ways to understand people and get along better with others are also covered in the book.

Books for Parents and Children to Share

Ages 4–6

Shooting Stars, by Franklyn M. Branley. Explains what a falling star is, its origin, what it is made of, and what happens when one lands on the earth or the moon.

Rain and Hail, by Franklyn M. Branley. Presents the water cycle that provides our earth with rain. Explains vapor condensation so that children can understand what makes rain and hail.

Things That Go, by Seymour Reit. Each letter of the alphabet is shown in upper and lower case along with a word for a vehicle that begins with that letter. Each vehicle is illustrated and described.

The Caterpillar Who Turned into a Butterfly (A Chubby Board Book). Shows, in simple terms, with colorful illustrations, how a caterpillar changes into a butterfly. Pages are thick and easy for young children to turn by themselves.

Do You Want to Be My Friend? by Eric Carle. A lonely little mouse is looking for a friend. He meets a horse, alligator, lion, peacock, monkey, fox, and several other animals before finding a fellow mouse.

The Ear Book, by Al Perkins. Shows what a dog and his friend can hear with their ears. They listen to people and animals, things inside and outside, and even food!

Ages 6–8

Why I Cough, Sneeze, Shiver, Hiccup, & Yawn, by Melvin Berger. Introduces the body's nervous system, including the spinal cord, brain, and nerves. Shows how reflexes happen and how they work through the nervous system.

The Berenstain Bears' Science Fair, by Stan and Jan Berenstain. The bears are having a science fair and are going to learn about machines, matter, and energy. They show how to do some science projects and experiments.

Eclipse, by Franklyn M. Branley. Explains what a solar eclipse is and how it happens. Shows how to safely watch an eclipse, and gives examples of stories people used long ago to explain this rare event.

Desert Life, by Ruth Kirk. Describes temperature, weather, animal and plant life, location, and landscape of a desert. Large illustrations accompany each topic.

Down Come the Leaves, by Henrietta Bancroft. Shows why leaves fall in autumn, what their role is for the tree, and how buds develop into new leaves in the spring. Gives examples of different kinds of trees and their leaves.

Fossils Tell of Long Ago, by Aliki. Tells what a fossil is, the different ways in which fossils can be made, and how to make one-minute-old fossils.

Ages 8–10

How to Do a Science Project, by David Webster. Gives suggestions for reporting, demonstrating, and researching science projects. Lists how-to-steps for a successful project.

The Sunlit Sea, by Augusta Goldin. An introduction to the underwater world. Describes marine plants and animals and shows how they depend on one another.

Tut's Mummy: Lost and Found, by Judy Donnelly. Depicts the burial of pharaoh Tutankhamen.

Recounts the discovery of his tomb and many treasures by archaeologists. Illustrated by photographs and drawings.

Junior Science Book of Water Experiments, by Rocco V. Feravolo. Discusses what water is, how it seeks its own level, and how water pressures and water power work. Gives examples of water experiments kids can do at home.

How Big is a Brachiosaurus? by Susan Carroll. Suggests possible answers to questions about dinosaurs and what dinosaurs might have looked like. Gives information about dinosaur fossils that have been found.

Science Club Super Motion, by Philip Watson. Most of the happenings on earth involve motion of some kind. By trying some of the experiments in this book, children can get a better idea of motion, vibrations, balance, and natural rhythm.

Learning Math at Home

Recently we had to build some storage shelves at work to hold the boxes of books and paper that were cluttering our work space. So we measured the wall where the shelves would be placed and then figured out how much lumber we would need. After that we called the lumber yard to estimate the cost of our project. All that measuring, figuring, and estimating were parts of a real-life math problem. We all do those kinds of math problems everyday.

Though often feared by students, math is probably our most frequently used school subject. We solve math problems when we ask: How many are going to eat lunch? How many bowls do we need? Spoons? Susie is having milk . . . Dad, coffee . . . Mom and Jake, water." We use math skills when we:

❖ Note likenesses and differences.
❖ Ask questions like, "Can you find a spoon like this one?" or "Can you locate the sweater with the square neck?"
❖ Estimate the time it will take to finish homework.

Think for a moment about the routine things that involve math:
❖ Setting the alarm to get up at a specified time.
❖ Measuring coffee for breakfast.
❖ Leaving for the bus with enough time to reach the bus stop.
❖ Sorting the laundry into piles, measuring detergent, setting the dials on the washer and dryer, and folding the clothes.

❖ Cooking meals.
❖ Paying bills.
❖ Using sales coupons.
❖ Discussing the family budget.
❖ Making phone calls.

So don't let anyone tell you or your child that math is too difficult for you. You do it all the time.

At home, then, you can help your child build self-confidence by making her aware of the math all around her. You can also help her see the relation between everyday math activities and school learning. There are three basic things that you can do:

First, help your child understand the problem. Remember the shelves we built? We could estimate the cost and order the lumber only after we measured the wall and figured out how much lumber those shelves required. In other words, we had to visualize the problem and lay it out step by step.

Second, help your child practice the base skills—addition, subtraction, multiplication, division, fractions, and decimals—so that the child can remember them and then use them correctly.

Third, help your child see patterns. Children need to see patterns in math and ways of organizing mathematical information. That's the great value of trying to put some information into an equation. The equals sign (=) helps children see the pattern of thinking that enables one side of the equation to match the other.

Problem Solving

In recent years, problem-solving has been emphasized in mathematics instruction. One study suggests that early childhood is a critical time to get a child ready for problem solving. Children can profit from activities that encourage them to explore their environment mathematically and to build a network that promotes problem solving.

Problem-solving strategies that parents can use to help their children understand math include:

- ❖ Rereading the problem.
- ❖ Looking for key words and ideas.
- ❖ Solving a similar (but easier) problem first.
- ❖ Looking for key words or phrases.
- ❖ Writing down important information.
- ❖ Making a list, a table, or a chart to organize the information
- ❖ Using a picture or objects to make the problem more real.

You might be interested in some other basic skill areas that have been identified by the National Council of Supervisors of Mathematics:

1. Being aware of the "reasonableness" or logic of results.

Children should learn to evaluate or inspect their results and check for reasonableness. If they were asked to find one-third of the length of a bedroom and their answer was 75 feet, is that a reasonable answer? Because calculators are now cheaper and more available, this is a skill all the more important.

2. Estimating answers.

Children should be encouraged to estimate some answers. They should acquire some simple techniques for estimating quantity, length, distance, weight, and so on. You can help your children by asking them to estimate room size, distance across your yard, or the weight of their baby brother. Children who can estimate are able to reject unreasonable answers to a problem and know when they are "in the ballpark."

3. Geometry.

Children should learn the geometric concepts—shapes, differences, parallels, perpendicular, line, point, and so on. These properties relate to measurement and problem-solving skills. Children must be able to recognize similarities and differences among objects.

4. Measurement.

Children should be able to measure distance, weight, time, capacity, and temperature. Children should be aware of measurement in both metric and standard systems and should use the appropriate tools.

5. Reading, interpreting, and constructing tables, charts, and graphs.

Children should understand time schedules, weather reports, and wage and income tables, which are all part of our daily lives.

6. Using math to predict.

Children should become familiar with how math is used to help make predictions. This is called probability. What's the probability that tomorrow mom will say, "OK, Henry, its time to get up for school"? Well, how often has she said it in the past? Every day? Then the probability is 100% that she will say it tomorrow.

7. Computer literacy.
Children should be aware of the many uses of computers in society. Encourage your child to take advantage of computer learning at school and at home, if you can afford one there.

What Can Parents Do?

As is the case with all school learning, parents can be valuable assets in helping their children develop math skills. The easiest and most direct way is just to talk about the math activities that occur daily. We have listed many of them in this section. Encourage your children to explore and to show their curiosity by asking questions like: how many pieces of candy do you think are in that dish? How can we measure the size of the ball without using a tape measure? How many pieces of paper will we need to wrap that big box?

When parents provide the materials and let the child do the activity, they encourage their child to take risks as a thinker. Learning math at home begins with something the child can touch and feel, like pennies and nickels, or a dark box full of newborn kittens, or storage boxes that have to fit precisely so they will all fit on the shelf. As the child realizes that math is used all around him, math may then make better sense in school and elsewhere. Please remember that math begins with the concrete experience. With sticks and blocks and measuring tape, your child will learn to handle math and feel comfortable with it.

Questions about Math

Math is a subject children need help with, and often parents are anxious or intimidated by this topic. Here are answers to some questions which will enable you to help your kids.

❓ **Our child has difficulty understanding money and making change. Do you have any suggestions to motivate him to learn this?**

Many families put extra change in a jar or container. If you have extra change or your child has money in his piggy bank, bring it out and let him use real money to practice making change. For example, ask your child to sort the change or coins into groups that equal a dollar; then count the groups. Remind him that this can be done by using what he already knows—counting by twos, fives, and tens.

Start out with simple sorting tasks, such as counting out enough dimes, quarters, or nickels to equal a dollar. Not only does this help your child learn how many dimes, quarters, or nickels equal a dollar, but it enables him to understand the value of each coin a little better. Once your son understands the value of coins and paper money then you can move on to problems and activities that involve counting out the correct amount of money or making change.

It is unreasonable to expect your son to do these calculations in his head right away. Adults who are dealing with money every day don't even do it—they use calculators and computer cash registers for that! When you give your son money problems at home, give him some paper and pencil to figure out the problem. Then ask him to count out the right amount of change.

As your son becomes more skilled at working with money, try challenging him. When you are shopping, ask him how much the two or three items you have in your shopping cart will cost. Have him add up the coupons you are going to use and let him tell you how much money will be saved. When shopping, or at a fast food place, ask your son to tell you how much change you should get back from the cashier. If your son gives the right answer, he gets to keep the coins!

❖ **I'm not good at math. I want our child, who isn't in school yet, to have a good attitude about math. What can I do with her before she gets to school that can avoid some of the problems and bad feelings that I have about math?**

Math plays a very important role in today's world of advanced technology. As a parent, you can help your child master the subject of mathematics. Even at a very early age, your child is able to use simple mathematical ideas, and you can increase her chances of success by providing suitable activities to develop these ideas.

Math is learned naturally by the inventive, curious mind. Pre-schoolers are easy and confident with numbers. They love to count and use counting a number of ways. By the time they enter kindergarten, they have many practical—but informal—math skills. For example, they can deal comfortably with situations requiring an idea of what is largest, smallest, tallest, longest, inside, outside, closest, farthest, and the like. They can do simple addition and subtraction by counting and looking at actual objects—apples, pencils, books, and so forth. They can correctly count to 10.

Help your child learn to count by using rhymes such as "one, two, buckle my shoe, three, four, shut the door." Read books to your child that involve counting. For example, *Over In the Meadow* or *The Three Little Pigs*. When reading aloud to her, ask her how many people, dogs, or whatever she sees in the picture.

Turn simple jumping, clapping, and hopping activities into counting activities. When doing work around the home, have her count out the objects. For instance, while setting the table have her count the plates, silverware, and napkins that are needed for dinner. Let her figure out how many potatoes you will need for dinner and then let her get them for you.

Make sure that "home" math has a noticeable problem-solving flavor. It should contain a challenge or question that can be answered. Ask your child how many pennies she has in her piggy bank. Have her take some away and then ask her again how many she has. Don't make the problems difficult—start with small numbers and simple problems so she can gain confidence in handling numbers and solving problems.

Reward your child with praise for correct answers. This helps build the child's confidence in problem-solving. Don't tell your child that some people are "no good" in math. Never tell your child you are "no good" in math, no matter how low your opinion is of your own skills! And by all means, don't think that girls aren't as good in math as boys.

❖ **I don't want to invest a lot of money in buying math things (games, flash cards, counters, beads, etc.) like they have at school. What can I use at home that can provide my children with the same math experiences?**

Math doesn't have to be an expensive investment to provide for stimulating experiences at home. Use objects that your children can touch, handle, and move. Researchers call these things "manipulatives." You have all sorts of these "manipulatives" all around the house!

They include familiar objects such as the miniature figures, cars, marbles, and so forth that young children play with. Some children have collections of shells or baseball cards. Use these items to make story problems for your children to solve or to use as counters instead of counting toes and fingers! Snacks, such as popcorn, raisins, M & M's, cereal, grapes, carrot sticks, and marshmallows make good things to count, and when you are done or get the problem right—you can eat them as a reward!

The plastic packaging called "peanuts" that many items are shipped in, old buttons, tooth picks, and paper clips make great things to use for solving math problems. Store them in a place your children can easily get to them.

Use old decks of cards for making your own set of flash cards. Write the basic facts on these old cards just as store-bought flash cards are designed. Cut up old birthday, Christmas, or greeting cards to make flash cards.

If you have dice around the house, use a pair of dice or several dice to practice math facts. Roll the dice and add them up. The one with highest or lowest score wins! If you don't have dice, you can make your own. Get a small piece of wood and cut it into small blocks. Write a number on each side of the block and you are ready to roll!

Use the measuring cups and spoons you use at home to help with teaching fractions. Cutting apples, oranges, and other foods helps to demonstrate fractions — what a half, a quarter, or one-third really looks like.

Tangrams are different geometric shapes that introduce your child to geometry. When teachers use tangrams at school, ask your child's teacher if you can borrow these shapes. You can make your own tangrams at home by tracing the shapes on a vinyl place mat and cutting them out. They are just as good as the purchased ones that you borrowed from the teacher!

Let your children come up with some of their own ideas to use. Once you get an idea, the possibilities are endless.

Math Activities

Help your child with math at home by using one or two of the following activities. Read through the ones listed below and select the appropriate ones to do with your children.

Shapes

Draw a circle or square or triangle, or use yarn to make the figure. Show it to your child and introduce the name of the shape. Send your youngster on a search for items in the house that have the same shape.

Sports Math

Review word problems with your child by using the basketball scores in the paper. Example: 30 games played; 12 wins. How many losses? 20 wins and 7 losses. How many games played?

How Far Is . . . ?

Help your child estimate how long it would take for her to walk to a specified location. Then take the walk and determine if your predictions were correct.

Let's Go Shopping

Play a shopping game. First have your child select ten items from a catalog. Then have him add the prices to figure out the total cost of the items. Next have him pretend he will receive a certain weekly allowance. Help him figure how long it would take to earn enough money to buy the selected items.

Books for Parents

Brain Building, by Karl Albrecht. Teaches seven steps to help foster clear thinking in problem solving and logic. Gives examples of problems and how to solve them step by step. Also presents games and puzzles to enhance problem-solving skills.

Family Math, by Jean Kerr Stenmark, Virginia Thompson, and Ruth Cossey. Presents ideas to help children (ages 5–18) learn math at home. Includes hands-on materials that focus on logical reasoning, problem solving, geometry, statistics, calculators, money, time, spatial thinking, probability, and measurement.

Math for Smarty Pants, by Marilyn Burns. Suggests activities and games that focus on everyday things to help children understand math. Covers geometry, logic, statistics, problem solving, and numeration.

Help Your Child Learn Number Skills, by Frances Mosley and Susan Meredith. Shows parents how to explore math with their children through play. Gives practical math activities to do at home to help children with their math skills. Covers number skills, shape, measurement, calculators, computers, and mental arithmetic.

Books for Parents and Children to Share

Ages 4–6

Annie's One to Ten, by Annie Owen. Illustrates different combinations of numbers that add up to ten. Uses a variety of related objects to count. Includes zero.

Shapes, by John J. Reiss. Presents a shape and then demonstrates familiar objects with that same shape. Creates new figures by manipulating basic ones. Shows squares, triangles, circles, cubes, pyramids, and spheres.

The Magic Clock, by Roger Burrows. Jane finds a magic clock that takes her to different places each time she turns the hands. Relates what time it is in words to the face of the clock.

Big Ones Little Ones, by Tana Hoban. Photos of mature animals with their young illustrate the concept of big and little. Lists different kinds of animals in the back of the book.

The Fancy Dress Party Counting Book, by John Patience. Shows groups of children in costume arriving at a birthday party. Includes numerals one through ten with children and counting dots. Includes simple story-problem questions.

Shapes, Shapes, Shapes, by Tana Hoban. A photographic collection of familiar objects seen every day. Shapes to look for are in the beginning of the book and appear throughout the photos. Includes arcs, circles, hearts, stars, ovals, squares, triangles, and more.

Ages 6–8

If You Made a Million, by David M. Schwartz. Describes the concepts of million, billion, and trillion by considering ways money can be spent. Delightful illustrations accompany text.

Anno's Math Games, by Mitsumasa Anno. Demonstrates concepts of multiplication, sequence, measurement, and direction. Discover the answers to given problems by looking closely at accompanying illustrations.

What Is Symmetry? by Mindel and Harry Sitomer. Explains symmetry and gives examples of symmetry in nature and manufactured products. Explores ways to test for line and point symmetry, and also covers plane symmetry. Gives instructions for making symmetrical patterns.

How Much Is a Million? by David M. Schwartz. Marvelosissimo, the mathematical magician, takes a journey and defines large numbers using familiar things. Depicts concepts of million, billion, and trillion through captivating illustrations.

Meet the Computer, by Seymour Simon. Discusses and explains a computer and how it works. Uses cartoons to illustrate the text.

Dollars and Cents for Harriet, by Betsy Maestro. Harriet is a hard-working elephant trying to earn enough money for a kite. Follow her and learn how different coins add up to make one dollar.

Ages 8–10

Anno's Hat Tricks, by Mitsumasa Anno and Akihiro Nozaki. Presents deductive reasoning through illustrated word puzzles. The reader must look at the "if" and determine the "then."

Anno's Mysterious Multiplying Jar, by Mitsumasa and Masaichiro Anno. Helps the reader visualize factorials through a story. Shows the use of the exclamation point: 3! for example, means $3 \times 2 \times 1$. This tale goes all the way to ten. Also examines factorials as a means to determine alternate orders of a set.

The Problem Solvers, by Nathan Aaseng. Discover the importance of problem-solving by looking at some successful products and companies. The inventions described in this book were created as solutions to problems. Discusses John Deere, Jacuzzi, Gerber, Polaroid, Evinrude, and others.

The I Hate Mathematics Book! by Marilyn Burns. Learn math by having fun with games, puzzles, riddles, and magic tricks. Covers numerology, probability, symmetry, logic, fractions, multiplication, and more.

Which One Is Different? by Joel Rothman. Twenty-six puzzles that challenge the best observation skills. Each page contains a set of objects, and one object is different from the others. Covers a variety of difficulty levels.

The Domino Book, by Frederick Berndt. Outlines puzzles and games to play using dominoes. Gives rules and versions of games from simple to complex. Can be played by children and adults.

Making History
Come Alive

When I was a boy, we used all kinds of jingles to remember important events in history—for instance: "In 1492 Columbus sailed the ocean blue" and "In 1865 Lincoln kept the Union alive."

Did you do things like that, too? Most of us use little tricks like that to help us remember important dates and events.

Though the approach to teaching history has changed since I was in elementary school, today's children still study major events in American history because they represent American culture. Columbus and other explorers, the Pilgrims, the Revolutionary War, the war between the North and the South, the abolition of slavery, and the Great Depression of the 1930s all had a significant impact on American life, as did many other events. Knowing about those moments in American history, then, gives children a sense of participation in the drama of the United States of America. This knowledge also connects them with the adults of the community. They have a common knowledge about their country.

But history is more than a simple record of past activities. History is an interpretation of those events and the people who participated in them. It is an attempt to explain why problems occurred and why people reacted to them as they did. For instance, why did we fight the Revolutionary War with Great Britain? And why did some colonists remain faithful to Britain while their neighbors fought against them? The answer to those questions calls for an interpretation of events, not simply a knowledge that the war happened. You can help your child with the study of history by showing them the difference between a knowledge of facts and constructing a story that interprets the facts.

History as Exploration

The word "history" comes from a Greek word meaning "inquiry" or exploring ideas. That emphasizes the notion that history means telling a story about the past that tries to explain why people act the way they do.

❖ Why did the Pilgrims come to America? They came here so they could practice their religion without interference.

❖ Why did we revolt against Great Britain? We did not want to be taxed without having elected representatives involved in the process.

❖ Why did we fight a civil war? The North wanted a strong federal government, and the South wanted to protect the self-determination of individual states, especially where slavery was concerned.

❖ How did the Great Depression of the 1930s change the United States? It made the federal government responsible for the social welfare of all its citizens.

With those four questions we have touched one major event in each of the past four centuries. The answers are my interpretations, but they are fairly common answers, so I guess they are safe ones. Having safe answers, however, doesn't do justice to the process of creating a story that you as an individual can understand. That's why many teachers now get their young students to read library books about people who lived through the events. They want to help children gain a concrete sense of what happened, rather than simply listing names and dates for which children have no feeling.

As adults, we each have a sense of past time. Our minds have developed to the point that we can comprehend changes that occurred over the centuries. Young children, on the other hand, have very little sense of the past. For all they know, George Washington, Abraham Lincoln, Franklin Roosevelt, and their own grandfather all lived about the same time. One researcher estimates that a first-grade child can hold one week in mind as her sense of the past. A sixth grader may be able to hold one year in mind for a sense of the past. That's because they can only relate the past to their own experience. Their minds haven't developed enough for them to lift themselves above their own experience to envision the development of people and nations one century ago or three thousand years ago.

When one of my daughters was young, she frequently asked me to tell her about the olden days. What she meant was tales from her father's childhood where he pitched hay, climbed trees to hide, and brought baby snakes to school to make everyone squeal. In my daughter's mind, I am sure that my childhood was all part of a world where dragons roamed the countryside and Indians danced in anger over the white man who invaded his hunting grounds. But that's all right. Young children need stories to give them a sense of a life and a time different from their own. Gradually, they will begin to sort out the sequence of past events.

My six-year-old nephew once asked my wife if there were dinosaurs when she was born. Naturally, I won't let my wife forget that question. In reply, however, we took one of his toy dinosaurs and placed it in one corner of the room. In the middle of the room we placed a picture of a naked bushman from the National Geographic magazine. In the opposite corner of the room we stood my wife. With that visual representation we tried to show my nephew that there was a huge amount of time between my wife, early man, and the dinosaur. And he concluded with the statement: "Oh, so there weren't dinosaurs even when Grandpa was born." He was on the right track.

You can do similar demonstrations with major historical events if they come up for discussion in your house. Those demonstrations won't give your child an immediate understanding of history, but they lay the groundwork for his mind to begin to separate events into historical sequence. These examples of my daughter and my nephew should reinforce the notion that concrete stories and activities about historical personalities and events are an important first step towards making them seem real. Across the years, your child will learn to sequence these events as it becomes necessary for him or her to formulate a comprehensible story, especially in school.

If you want to help your child develop a sense of history, probably the place to start is your own family.

Why not have your child ask grandparents or older relatives for their favorite stories from the past? One second-grade teacher in Louisiana had her students learn a little about their family's history by having the older people in the family dictate stories to these second graders. Some came back with stories about their parents; some about grandparents; some about great-grandparents. Here are samples of the stories these seven-year-olds brought back to read to their classmates:

The Headless Rabbit!!

Once upon a time, in the mountains of Alabama, my great-grandfather was going to visit a sick friend. There were no roads or cars, so he was walking on a trail across the mountain. It was beginning to get dark when he saw a figure coming toward him. Since he was a hunter and not afraid of things in the woods, he decided to wait on the trail for the approaching creature. It looked like a white rabbit, but as it brushed past his leg he realized the rabbit had no head or tail. He turned and watched as the rabbit hopped out of sight.

When Great-Grandfather got to his friend's house, he learned his friend had passed away about the same time he had seen the rabbit on the trail. He wondered if the two events were related.

You may find this story hard to believe, but my great-grandfather wasn't a drinking man and always told the truth.

He lived to be 72 years old and said this was the only thing he ever saw that he couldn't explain.

(This story was told to me by my grandmother about her father and occurred about 1910 in Scottsboro, Alabama.)

Tongue Twister

Once upon a time, when my father was a boy, he lived in South Dakota.

One winter day, my father and my uncle were outside in the freezing cold. My father said to my uncle, "Let's put our tongues on the car bumper and lick off the frost."

"Good idea!" said my uncle.

"You go first," said my dad.

So, my uncle touched his tongue to the cold, frosty bumper, and it stuck.

My uncle couldn't get his tongue off. He said, "AAAHHHGGG!"

My dad said, "What's the matter, brother?"

"AAAHHHGGG!" said my uncle again, still stuck to the bumper.

"I better get help," my dad said. He ran into the house to his father. "Dad, Dad, Dick is stuck to the car! Come quick!"

"What?"

"Come quick and see."

They rushed outside and found my uncle on his knees, his tongue stuck to the bumper.

"What are you doing?" his father shouted.

"AAAHHHGGG!" said my uncle.

Then his father got a pan of warm water and poured it on my uncle's tongue. Slowly my uncle's tongue peeled off the bumper.

"Are you crazy?" said his father.

My uncle pointed his finger at my dad and said, "He made me do it!"

For several days afterwards, my uncle and my dad were sore in different places.

Aren't those wonderful stories? By collecting stories from their own families these second graders had a peek into the past. They uncovered a story that gave them a concrete sense of the past. Years later they will interpret those stories differently because they will understand more clearly the times in which they occurred—in other words, they will have a clearer sense of history.

What Parents Can Do

There are several other specific activities parents can do with their children to help them understand history better. Here are a few of them.

Family Artifacts

Think of a list of items to put in a time capsule to be opened a thousand years from now. First, compile a list of some things that your family owns, including items from each room in the house. Then, select those items that would provide the most information about your family and would be of interest to people in the distant future.

Family Tree

Help children start their own family tree. If the family already has a genealogical tree, it can be used to help make and design their own. The tree might include pictures of each family member and give information such as birth date, death date, or nickname.

Photo Album

Get out old photo albums that show pictures of family members who are a part of the children's past but who died before they were born. Also, show children pictures of themselves and their parents when they were young.

Share Books

Read stories with settings that take place during various times in history. These might be historical fiction novels or biographies of famous people who lived in the past. Talk about how these peoples' lives were different from our own and what the advantages and disadvantages would be of living in those times.

Songs

Teach your children songs or chants that tell about life in the past. Children will learn that many songs were written to tell about the feelings of the people of specific times. Songs that parents learned when they were little, folk songs, work songs, songs about particular events, and nursery rhymes can all provide information about how people lived in the past. For example, there is an interesting history behind such songs as "Yankee Doodle Dandy" and "Star Spangled Banner," songs that grew out of slavery like "Go Down, Moses," and nursery rhymes like "Rub-a-Dub-Dub" or "Sing a Song of Sixpence."

Community Helpers

Visit a police station or fire station and talk to the women and men who work there about their jobs. Look at their equipment, and talk about how the equipment and the job have changed over their work lives. Then, visit a library and check out books that explain how police or fire stations operated in the past. Talk about how these jobs have changed over the years and about the advantages of modern equipment.

School Yearbook

Have your children start a yearbook that includes pictures of them each year and tells their height, weight, classes they liked, special awards they received, and special activities in which they were involved. This book can be looked at to see how they have changed physically, socially, and mentally over time. Later, after they are grown up, this yearbook will be a source of memories and enjoyment.

Folk Medicine

To help children understand how the medical world has changed, talk about folk medicine. Tell them about some remedies that their grandparents used to cure sickness. Check out a book from the library about folk medicine, or about cures used by early pioneers to cure illnesses or heal injury. For example, here are a few silly ones: to cure a sore throat, some pioneers tied the right front foot of a mole around their neck with a black thread. If they had a sty in their eye, they would run the tip of a black cat's tail over it. For a toothache, they rubbed their gums with rattlesnake rattles or the brain of a rabbit. For headaches, they rubbed onions on their brows. There is also a lot of common sense and wisdom in folk medicine. It can be cheaper than modern medicine, too. Have your children ask older people in the family or among your friends about effective home remedies they have known or used.

Visit a Cemetery

Visit cemeteries where your ancestors are buried. Read the epitaphs on the tombstones and reconstruct the family relationships of those buried together.

Visit Museums

Take your children to historical, art, or children's museums. Museums that have people dressed in clothing of a particular period, carrying out everyday tasks such as carpentry, shoemaking, and cooking, are a wonderful way for children to experience different periods in time.

Family History Project

Most children have questions about who they are. They like to know about their roots, their personal backgrounds. One way to discover why they behave in certain ways and not in others, or why they believe in certain things and not in others, is to examine their family's past. Attitudes and belief systems were developed in some family context. Interviews with relatives (grandparents, aunts, uncles, cousins, and others) are a way to find out about the family's past. If they live far away, either call or write them to get the information. How far back do the stories in your family go?

Almanac

Buy or check out from the library a copy of the *Farmer's Almanac*. This publication has been produced continuously since 1792 and is full of history. The recipes, predictions, and information have been used by Americans for nearly 200 years. Look at the book together and find out what types of information it provides. Talk about how this publication might have been used in the 1790s. Why would it have been useful to people living on farms in isolated areas of the country? Why would this book be useful today?

Crafts

Crafts in colonial times were much different from ours today. In many instances, the materials used to make these crafts were different as well. Check out books from the library on pioneer or colonial crafts and try making some of them together. These crafts might include such things as candle making or making children's toys.

With these ideas, you can help make history come alive for your children.

Activities for Fun and Learning

History often seems abstract to children because they cannot experience it in a tangible way. Try some of the following activities with your children to make history come alive for them.

❖ Use family photographs to show your children what their ancestors' lives were like. This will help them better understand their origins and their world as it has evolved.

❖ Read about the hypothetical and historical discoveries of America by sharing *The Discovery of the Americas* by Betsy and Giulio Maestro. This book describes ventures of Stone Age hunters, the Phoenicians, the Vikings, Columbus, Cabot, and Magellan. After reading the book, help your children make a time line so they can see the chronological order of these events.

❖ Cook up some edible history with your kids. Share *Little House on the Prairie* by Laura Ingalls Wilder or *Little Women* by Louisa May Alcott. Then use *The Little House Cookbook* or *The Louisa May Alcott Cookbook* to prepare some of the recipes you read about in one of the stories. You can discuss ingredients, cooking methods and equipment, customs, clothing, and architecture, and relate them to the time period of the story.

❖ Help your child learn about a particular time in the past. Together, select and investigate a year. Look for books, photographs, clothes, records, TV programs, cars, and other signs of that time to observe what it was like "back then."

Books for Parents

Eyeopeners! How to Choose and Use Children's Books about Real People, Places, and Things, by Beverly Kobrin. A guide to over 500 nonfiction books. An easy-to-use index aids in location of books about history. Also includes tips for book selection, book-based activities, and ideas to nurture reading.

The Wild Shores: America's Beginnings, by Tee Loftin Snell. Elaborates on America's early exploration and colonization. Artwork of the time, maps, paintings, and photographs support the text. This book covers the years 1492 through 1841.

Chronicle of America, Clifton Daniel, editorial director. Presents history as news by using a newspaper-style format. Divides history into eight segments: 1) A New World, B.C.–1606; 2) Conceived in Liberty, 1607–1763; 3) Harvest of Freedom, 1764–1788; 4) A Perfect Union? 1789–1849; 5) A House Divided, 1850–1877; 6) Yearning to Breathe Free, 1878–1916; 7) Saving the Dream, 1917–1945; and 8) The Eagle Ascendant, 1946–1988. Abundant illustrations supplement the concise articles.

1,001 Things Everyone Should Know about American History, by John A. Garraty. Reviews American history from 1704 up to the late 1980s by noting important ideas, people, and places pertaining to politics, literature, music, presidents, economics, and military matters. Black and white photographs and drawings illustrate the text.

Books for Parents and Children to Share

Ages 4–6

All Those Secrets of the World, by Jane Yolen. Describes homecomings and furloughs that occurred during World War II. Lyrical text and splendid watercolor illustrations make this book perfect for reading aloud. Gives parents or grandparents an opportunity to talk about the war without using harsh text and brutal pictures.

Cowboys, by Glen Rounds. Presents the work and fun of a cowboy's life through amusing pictures and brief text. Shows kids a way of life that is relatively unknown.

The Buck Stops Here: The Presidents of the United States, by Alice Provensen. Depicts the first 41 American presidents through poster-style format using rhymed verse and full-page illustrations. This book serves as an entertaining and educational way to introduce the presidents to children.

Shaker Lane, by Alice and Martin Provensen. Describes folks who live on Shaker Lane and their lifestyles. When a reservoir is built on their property, the residents of this rural community lose their homes to suburban development. This story provides a glimpse of a trend found in American society—destroying rural, less wealthy areas to create suburbs for those more prosperous.

When I Was Young in the Mountains, by Cynthia Rylant. Relates fond memories of a young girl's Appalachian childhood through amusing, yet loving, text and warm paintings. Children can observe a way of life from another era and sample a bit of Appalachian culture.

Ages 6–8

The Oregon Trail, by Leonard Everett Fisher. Portrays life during western expansion by using journals, photographs and historical documents. Features the people who migrated westward and captures their hopes and fears. Westward expansion becomes more real to children when they look at these authentic people and records.

New Providence, by Jorg Muller. A series of detailed paintings shows some changes that have transpired in an American town over several years. Children can compare the pictures, discuss changes they notice, what those changes imply, and then reflect upon the pros and cons of ethical matters represented.

Scholastic Inc., publishes a series of small paperbacks which recount different events and periods in American history. These books relate historical events to the society, politics, government, and customs that shaped them. They help children understand the causes and effects of important historical episodes. Some of the titles include the following:

If You Lived at the Time of Martin Luther King, by Ellen Levine
If You Lived in Colonial Times, by Ann McGovern
If You Sailed on the Mayflower, by Ann McGovern
If You Traveled on the Underground Railroad, by Ellen Levine
If You Traveled West in a Covered Wagon, by Ellen Levine
If You Were There When They Signed the Constitution, by Elizabeth Levy

Jean Fritz is a popular author of biographies that focus on American history. Children enjoy reading these historically accurate stories. Some of her books include the following:

And Then What Happened, Paul Revere?
Can't You Make Them Behave, King George?
The Double Life of Pocahontas
Make Way for Sam Houston
What's the Big Idea, Ben Franklin?

Ages 8–10

A 19th Century Railway Station, by Fiona Macdonald. The 19th century was a time of great change in America, and the railroad created some of that change. While focusing on trains and stations, children learn about the broader impact railroads had on the country during this time period.
Lyddie, by Katherine Paterson. Lyddie takes a job in a factory to help her family get out of debt and regain their farm. She may lose everything be-

cause she is willing to take a stand concerning her terrible working conditions. Through the eyes of this likeable character, children can see the effect of industrialization on society.

Nothing to Fear, by Jackie French Koller. This is a story about the Depression from the perspective of a young boy. It touches on the discouragement and hopelessness people experienced during this period in United States history. Readers also encounter the determination, bravery, and generosity that enabled communities to survive.

Poetry of the First World War, selected by Edward Hudson. Writings of well-known as well as obscure poets invoke a powerful, stirring image of war. Presents, through verse and photographs, feelings of patriotism, disillusionment, resignation, anger, and fear. Deals with war, not by using a textbook filled with governments, dates, and places, but by showing some of the people who were involved, and their thoughts and feelings. Indirectly poses the question, "Does anyone really win a war?"

A Separate Battle: Women and the Civil War, by Ina Chang. Most history books only focus on men and their actions. This book focuses on women and their experiences during the Civil War. Graphic accounts, photographs, diaries and letters tell stories of women forming aid societies, serving as spies and couriers, working as nurses, fighting against slavery, and supporting women's rights.

Pearl Harbor Is Burning! A Story of World War II, by Kathleen V. Kudlinski. Frank moves to Hawaii and becomes friends with a Japanese-American boy named Kenji. When the Japanese bomb Pearl Harbor, questions of allegiance and trust arise. Presents ordinary people who are part of history.

Using the Library

As you may know, some adults use the public library a lot and some don't use it at all. That fact may not worry you, but there is a hidden message about adult library users that is valuable for parents to know. Our reading and library habits as adults seem to grow out of the experiences we had as children. That's right, regular reading and regular use of the library by adults stems from early use of the library as children. Recent studies of adult reading habits remind us of the powerful influence early reading experiences have on us.

In a study of summer library use, researchers found some low-achieving students reading books all summer, contrary to expectations. Why did these poor readers keep reading at the library? Two major reasons: the library offered prizes (food coupons and movie passes) to children who read a certain number of books, and most importantly, the parents of these low-achieving readers insisted that they participate in the library summer reading program.

This study of a summer library program shows that if parents encourage their children to read, the children are likely to appreciate the value of books early on in their lives. If parents encourage their children to use the library as a resource, they are likely to view the library as an asset they can draw upon. The world of information in the library then becomes a treasure they can use the rest of their lives.

Libraries Reach Out

Libraries are becoming more attentive to the needs of modern society. A New York City Library opened an Early Childhood Resource and Information Center for children (ages 0–7), and their caregivers. For the convenience of its users, the Center made it a priority to install a diaper-changing station.

The librarians at these libraries combined their own experience and their knowledge of early literacy to implement a program just for parents and very young children. They built a space in the library that enabled parents and young children to share books together and to get help from librarians on selecting appropriate material. This same early childhood space made it possible for parents with limited English to practice their reading by using picture books with only a few words. Books with predictable phrases and sentences and books with word patterns, such as the Dr. Seuss books, were treasured by adults almost as much as they were by young children.

Librarians have a tradition of holding story hours for children in which they read some of their favorite stories. More and more, parents are being encouraged to read stories to their children by using the nooks and corners of the Children's Department as their own story corners.

A benefit of summer library programs is that the children who use them return to school in the fall with stronger reading skills than those who did not read much during the summer. If the library offers rewards to children for reading books, accept them graciously. Even though you may think that children should read books just for the joy of reading, your goal is to encourage them to read regularly. If rewards do that, let them roll. Once children begin to read regularly, they have a much better chance of becoming the habitual readers who succeed in school and in the jobs of the future.

Library Services for Preschoolers

In case you are wondering what the library offers besides stacks of books, here are a few examples of services that you can find for preschoolers:

❖ Many libraries have records and games that show you how to stimulate your child's language development through songs, games, and activities.

❖ The Children's Department will have lists of books on child rearing and parenting, as well as information about programs that the library organizes in these areas.

❖ Special demonstrations are offered to help parents learn how to use finger-plays, songs, rhymes, and other activities that stimulate language development, vocabulary, and concepts that are helpful in school.

❖ Children can often engage in activities such as listening to stories, watching films, doing arts and crafts work, and watching puppet shows, while their parents are using the library.

Be sure to take advantage of all the benefits that the library offers you as a parent of young children. As we have already mentioned, the long-term benefits for your child are immeasurable.

Library Services for School-age Children

Once your children are in school, the library becomes even more important. The public and school library then become an extension of the classroom. Although there are activities that encourage children to write and to participate in creative drama at the library, it is the information resources of the library that give children the power to learn beyond the limits of classroom activities.

Good teachers regularly challenge their students to use the library and other resources to expand classroom learning. Some expanded learning might be called recreational reading—reading for fun—but other learning involves children in finding topics that interest them and in becoming experts in those subjects.

Computers and information programs are frequently available at libraries. They give children an opportunity to search for answers to their questions and to solve problems by gathering information that will make them informed decision-makers.

Gifted and talented youngsters can enjoy the benefits of the library by joining discussion groups or by using the library as a warehouse of information to explore the ideas that are interesting to them. Children with physical or mental impairments may also benefit from special resources, such as books on tape and Braille print books, magazines, and comic books that are usually available free of charge.

Many libraries have tutors available or homework "helplines" for students to ask questions about their assignments. It is also common for libraries to house the local adult literacy program. So, if people need help with their literacy skills, this is probably the first place to go.

Parents' Resolutions

As you think about using the library to help your children become better readers and more effective students, it might be a good idea to rehearse in your mind the kinds of statements that you want to make about yourself as a way of being a model for your children. You may even want to print some of these statements on 3" x 5" cards as reminders of what you can do to help your children. Try some of the following statements to see if they represent your way of thinking:

- ❖ I have a library card and I get one for each of my children.

- ❖ I take my children to the library regularly.

- ❖ I make each trip to the library an exciting discovery.

- ❖ I make a special effort to read with my children.

- ❖ I help my children find books that they can bring home.

- ❖ I respect the choices of books that my children make.

- ❖ While my children are exploring the library, I spend time searching for books that fit my own needs.

- ❖ I am a model for my children.

When parents, teachers, and librarians work together, the literacy skills of their children are bound to improve and everyone will end up a winner.

Questions about the Library

If parents have not used a library frequently, sometimes it seems confusing. We would like to answer a few questions you might have concerning a library. These suggestions could make your next trip to a library more productive and enjoyable.

◈ I don't feel confident taking my child to the library. What do I need to know or understand about helping my child use the library?

There is no need to be intimidated by the library. Once you are inside, you will see that many people are just browsing or reading. You can feel comfortable looking around until you locate the information desk or librarian. Librarians will be happy to direct you to the children's department or to a source that will help you locate the books you want.

A library keeps a record of all its materials. You can locate materials in a library by using a card catalog or a computer. Cards in a card catalog are located in a series of drawers that are arranged in alphabetical order by author, title, or subject. If you are looking for a book by title and it begins with the word "A", or "The", move to the next word in the title. For example, *A Tree Grows in Brooklyn* would be filed under "**T**". Be sure to have a slip of paper and a pencil with you. When you locate the book you need, write down the NUMBER that appears on the top left hand corner of the catalog card, the title of the book, and the author. Notice the example we have provided for you below.

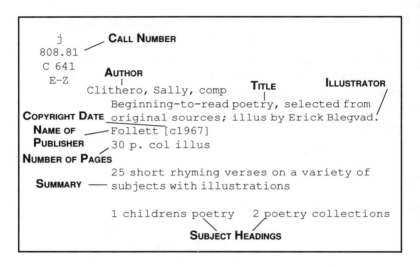

Some libraries have their catalog on computers. If your library has such a system, ask your librarian to show you how to use the computer to retrieve the information for which you are searching. Books are listed by author, title, or subject in the computer, also. Once you have used the computer to find books, you will see how much faster and easier it is to use than a card catalog.

Practice using the information you have learned. Make a trip to your library just to learn more about it. Pick a topic in which you and your child are interested. See what books you can find in the card catalog on this topic. Not only are you learning more about the library, but by including your child in this search process, you are helping your child learn how to use the library.

Once you and your child have found the information you want from the card catalog or computer, you should look for the book on the shelf. Typically, books are arranged in two ways. FICTION books are arranged alphabetically by the first letter of the author's last name. A book by Sidney Sheldon, for instance, will be on the "S" shelf. NONFICTION books are arranged by the call number. Remember, a call number for the book is written in the upper left-hand corner of the card. This same number can be found on the outside of the book so that it can be located on the shelf. We have provided another example on the following page to help you remember how different books are arranged in the library. You may find this picture helpful the next time you visit the library.

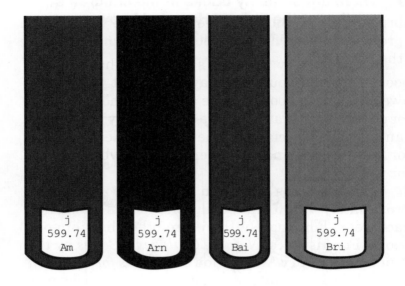

Another section of the library you should become familiar with is the reference area. Knowing how to find and use materials in this section will be helpful when your child is working on reports and term papers. The reference section of the library includes encyclopedias, atlases, government documents, and other types of information books. Reference books and documents in this section may not be checked out from the library.

There is more in your library than just books! Many libraries have newspapers, magazines, videos, tapes, records, computer software, and much more. The library is a living encyclopedia of useful information and materials, both past and present. Plan to use it for more than just fiction books. And remember, don't be afraid to ask for help when using the library. If you ask your librarian for help the first few times, you will soon find that the library is very easy to use.

❖ There are so many books in the children's section of the library. How do I know which books to choose?

Almost every children's librarian has lists of books to guide you. You may also want to look for award-winning books. There are two famous awards for children's literature made each year by the American Library Association. One is the Caldecott Medal for illustrations and the other is the Newbery Medal for writing.

These awards are given for only two of the approximately 2,500 new children's books published each year. Fortunately there are other lists of good books. For instance, *Notable Children's Books* by the American Library Association and *Books for Children* by the Library of Congress are lists of best books new for preschool through junior high school-aged children. The International Reading Association (IRA) publishes annual lists of books that children, teachers, and young adults recommend for reading. There are some excellent books to guide parents in book selection, such as *The New Read-Aloud Handbook* by Jim Trelease, *Comics to Classics: A Parent's Guide to Books for Teens and Preteens* by Arthea Reed, and *Eyeopeners* by Beverly Kobrin.

The children's librarian is trained to help you locate specific books that are good for reading aloud, as well as books on a particular subject recommended for a particular age group. In addition, your library may have several journals that regularly review children's books, including *The Horn Book*. Some of the family or parent magazines at the library, or the ones that you subscribe to at home, often recommend books for children.

❷ How can I help my child with school assignments, such as reports and term papers?

Very often children in school will ask their parents for help with library assignments. And very often parents will find themselves gradually taking over and doing a report for their son or daughter. Obviously, such an exercise offers no long-term benefit to your child. There are, however, things you can do to help your child with library assignments:

1) Ask your child questions about the assignment and encourage him to ask the teacher questions. This helps him to clarify what needs to be done. Help your child to identify the subtopic he is researching. For example, brontosaurus is a subgroup or smaller topic of dinosaurs, and dinosaurs is a subtopic of extinct animals. These classifications will help your child identify useful references.

2) Suggest that your child look up the topic in the library card catalog and in reference books. The librarian can also direct and help you get started. Be sure your child knows how to use a table of contents and an index. Suggest that she be prepared to look through or to use more than one source.

3) Help your child break assignments into logical segments and avoid last-minute panic by setting deadlines for each step of the work. Work together on setting up a schedule that allows plenty of time to gather needed materials.

4) Help your child decide if the community library has the resources he needs or if he should check other resources. He may want to talk to people who are experts on the topic; he may come up with ideas of his own as to where additional information can be obtained for the report.

5) Encourage your child to ask the librarian for help in locating materials. Help him gain confidence in using the library by letting him do his own talking when he needs help from the librarian.

6) Give your child encouragement, advice, and a ride if she needs it, but resist the temptation of taking over an assignment. Let her assume responsibility for researching and writing the report. It is the only way she will learn the library skills that she will need for the rest of her life.

Also, libraries frequently have workshops on how to do research or books reports. You may want to consider suggesting your child attend one of these workshops. But don't expect the library to fulfill your responsibilities as a parent.

Activities for Fun and Learning

Children usually enjoy learning when they participate in different activities. Use the following activities to help familiarize your child with a library and improve their library-related skills.

Alphabet Soup
To practice alphabetizing, have your child make a list of items in a room, or favorite foods, the names of players on a team, friends, or family. Then help her put them in alphabetical order.

Scavenger Hunt
At the library, select a title in the card catalog or on the computer, then show your child how to locate the item on the shelf. After he learns how to do this, challenge him to a game. Select a title and see if he can find it by himself. You may want to add a time limit as he improves.

Check It Out
There are activities available at most local libraries for children of all ages to enjoy. These activities include puppet shows, storytelling, workshops on writing reports and using computers, demonstrations, and booktalks.

Resources for Parents

Building a Family Library, by Reading Is Fundamental, Inc. $0.50 single copy, $15 per 100. This new brochure offers ideas for creating an economical family library. It also includes suggestions to help children build their own collections.

Helping Your Child Use the Library, Office of Educational Research and Improvement, U. S. Department of Education. Presents information about libraries, the services provided for children of all ages and adults, and strategies parents can use to help their children at the library.

The New York Times Parent's Guide to the Best Books for Children, edited by Eden Ross Lipson. Surveys a selection of children's books grouped according to reading levels. Annotations include author, illustrator, publisher, major awards, plot summary, and recommendations. Includes special indexes to help guide the user in locating appropriate books.

The Horn Book. Published six times a year, this journal contains reviews, articles and special columns about the best new books for children and young adults. For information, write: The Horn Book, Inc., 31 St. James Avenue, Boston, MA 02116–4167.

Notable Children's Books. For the most recent annual list, send $0.30 to: American Library Association, 50 East Huron Street, Chicago, IL 60611.

Books for Parents and Children to Share

Ages 4–6

There's a Cricket in the Library, by several fifth-grade students of McKee Elementary School in Oakdale, PA. This little cricket discovers books are for reading and not eating. He packs his things and leaves the library after being told to be quiet.

Blue Bug Goes to the Library, by Virginia Poulet. Blue Bug tours the library and learns about different materials, activities, and resources. Minimum amount of text on each page.

Ages 6–8

Good Books, Good Times, selected by Lee Bennett Hopkins. Entertaining illustrations accompany this collection of poems about books and the joy of reading.

Libraries, by Patricia Fujimoto. Covers the historical development of libraries and provides information about different types of libraries. Explains the services offered by libraries and suggests ways to use the library to find answers.

Hot Off the Press: Getting the News into Print, by Ruth Crisman. Describes the production of newspapers, from the publishing phase to delivery. Includes a glossary and a list of books for further reading.

A Visit to the Library, by Sylvia Root Tester. Follows a group of children on a tour of their local library. Introduces the use of library cards and care of books. Presents a variety of resources and activities that this library offers.

Dear Annie, by Judith Caseley. Grandpa sent Annie a card when she was born. Now Annie and her Grandpa are pen pals. They share their love for each other by sending cards and writing letters.

How a Book Is Made, by Aliki. Outlines the process of making and selling a book. Looks at the contributions of the author, illustrator, editor, publisher, designer, printer, salesperson, and many others.

Ages 8–10

Tracking the Facts: How to Develop Research Skills, by Claire McInerney. Covers selecting a topic, using the library, interviewing, and computer searching. Also provides information on taking notes, organizing an outline, and writing up research results.

Freedom of the Press, by J. Edward Evans. Gives a history of the freedom and restraint of the press. Covers the invention of the Gutenburg press to the Pentagon papers.

Books and Libraries, by Jack Knowlton. Illustrates the history and development of books and libraries from several early civilizations to the present.

Help Is on the Way for: Library Skills, by Marilyn Berry. Presents common operations and functions of a library. Focuses on general library rules and using a library card and card catalog. Suggests methods to locate different types of information.

Find It! The Inside Story at Your Library, by Claire McInerney. Explains the various resources and services available in a library. Provides information about recreational reading, different types of media, location and proper use of materials, and conducting research for school reports. Also includes humorous cartoons.

Making Writing Meaningful

Why do most school compositions get low or mediocre grades? Probably because most school compositions express low, mediocre thoughts.

If it is true that student compositions reflect a low level of thinking, then we have to conclude that students think dull thoughts; or, on the other hand, maybe students do not write about their exciting ideas in school compositions. Perhaps they are saving these exciting ideas for another time or are looking for another way to express them.

It is worthwhile for us to examine our children's writing because that's how they reveal their thoughts in school and later on the job. Teachers evaluate student progress from written exercises, and more and more jobs now require regular written reports.

A report from the National Assessment of Educational Progress shows that only one out of five American students can express herself adequately in writing. That leaves eighty percent of American children in the inadequate category——eighty percent cannot explain their thoughts or their feelings in writing.

What can you as a parent do about improving your children's writing skills? Actually quite a lot. The most important thing you can do is to act as an interested audience for the compositions your children write in school. As you read a school composition, you could say, "I understand that. That part is clear to me." Or, "This section is not clear to me. Is there another way you could describe this part so I can understand your thoughts?" Those kinds of comments show your children that you are reacting to their thoughts, praising clarity and asking questions when their thoughts are expressed in a jumbled way. And that's the first reaction any thoughtful reader has. Afterward, you can discuss things like punctuation and spelling if your child needs that kind of help at the moment.

Why Is Personal Writing Important?

All writing demands clarity of thought and a search for the right word to express those thoughts. That's where personal, reflective writing becomes valuable. A diary or a personal journal is an excellent vehicle for this kind of expressive writing. It gives children an opportunity to play with their thoughts and with their language. It gives them an experimental playground for their ideas. In a sense, they can show off for themselves, allow themselves the opportunity to test their skills and their strengths—just as children do on a playground—before they ask the advice of an adult. Learning how to communicate their thoughts and

feelings in personal writing encourages children to apply their expressive abilities to the more businesslike world of school reports, and compositions, and, later in life, to writing summaries or letters in the workplace.

Here are a couple of examples of children expressing their personal thoughts. Notice how their choice of words reflects their attempts to understand and interpret their experience.

The Prince Who Wanted A Girl

Once upon a time there lived a prince, a very sad prince, he wanted a princess to marry him. His father the king wanted for all the girls that came to take a test first, then if they passed it they would marry the prince. Well some of the girls passed some didn't, but the trouble was that the girls that passed the prince didn't like them. So his father grew tired of bringing girls that passed all very pretty and rich girls and one day as the prince was taking his royal ride on the royal stable with his royal horse he saw this very poor girl walking along the royal stable. She was very tired she didn't have no

shoes her clothes were ripped and she was very dirty. The prince got near her and asked "What's your name?" "I'm the prince of Europe my name is Alexander, would you like to marry me?" Then the girl said, "yes." So they got married, they bought her new clothes, Alexander became the king of Europe. And they became happily ever after.

The little girl who wrote this story lived in a very poor town near the Mexican border. If we read closely between the lines, we are able to figure out that this fairy tale is really about a little girl who wants a prince to rescue her from a difficult situation. The line "Once upon a time" expresses the little girl's belief that in a different time and place her life could be happier.

In the next essay, we see a very powerful example of a young boy attempting to come to grips with his mother's lifestyle.

My Dads

My mom was married when she was 18. Because she was pregnant with my older brother Steve. When Steve was about 4 years old Bob (my dad) used to beat him. And then she became pregnant with me. Which was an accedent. And when I was born Bob left us. Which really makes me feel good. I have only seen him about 10 times after he left.

Then a couple of years later she married Cal. I don't really remember that much of him.

My mom and brother say he used to beat me. But, he would come home drunk almost every night. And he smoked too. And my mom found out a lot of different but personal poroblems he had. And she could not cope with them. So they were devorced.I don't know how long it was But then she married Don. I didn't like him from the start. He was always mean to my mom, and he tried to hit her with a chair once. Ever since then I've really disliked him. She devorced him.

Then about 2 or 3 years later she married Ervin. I think thats how he spelled his name. I liked him. But just before they were married she found out some personal things about him. She picks some real winners. So she got an annulment.

So she dated for a while. And pretty soon Don was back. They dated off and on. One night they went out and when I woke up in the morning she wasn't home yet. Just before I left for school she called and said she was going to pick me up from school. And she told me her and Don had got married last night. So there I was stuck with a man I didn't like and my mom was married to him. But pretty soon Don was seeing some other girl so they got an annulment.

Now she's dating a lot of guys. And she says she's not going to marry for a long time. And only if its in the temple.

But I don't know what to believe what she says. In a way I think she aught to give up guys.

This young boy has had a lot of uncertainty and upheaval in his life. Notice how his use of phrases like "Then a couple of years later" and "I don't know how long it was" represents this boy's attempt to under-

stand disturbing experiences by organizing them into an historical perspective. Writing is a good outlet for him because it has allowed him to communicate his frustrations. This is one of the great advantages of self-expression. Can you imagine the conversation that might take place if this boy and his mother were to talk about how her lifestyle was affecting him? Writing can help your children express their feelings and thoughts in ways that can surprise you. You need to encourage them.

How Can Parents Encourage Their Children?

We, as parents, can help our children develop their abilities to express exciting, meaningful ideas in their writing. All writing requires time for preparation, time for drafting, and time for reviewing. If your children ask for your help or say they don't know what to write about, do some brainstorming with them.

Explore recent events in their lives, trips taken, movies seen, celebrations, or books they have read.

Choose one of the topics and ask them to think about how they felt, how it relates to their family or their friends, and what impressed them the most. They may want to jot down notes about this topic as you talk together. They may want to draw a picture to give the event a clearer focus in their minds. Perhaps they will share with you what the drawing means to them and why they chose some of the details in it.

Encourage your children to use that discussion and those notes or drawings while they are writing their thoughts and feelings. Maybe they want to tell a story about the topic or the event. A story plan might give them a sense of direction for keeping their ideas flowing.

After they have finished putting their ideas on paper, if they want you to work with them, talk to them about their writing. Unless their piece is quite personal, most children will relish feedback from their parents. They are hoping for encouragement, of course, but they also want to check out their ideas. Are their thoughts clear? Are they valuable? Will an adult appreciate their ideas? So when you are reading your child's expressive writing paper, remember to praise the clear ideas but also to identify those that are not clear to you. If the writing stems from a formal school assignment, your child may want you to look for other ways to improve the assignment.

Parent's Role

Here are a few quick guidelines that may help you work with your child:

❖ Provide a place in your home where your child can write comfortably.

❖ Be patient, and allow your child sufficient time to think and to write.

❖ Respond regularly to your child's writing, either in conversation or in writing.

❖ Be positive in discussing your child's writing. Praise what is clear and give suggestions for clarifying vague parts of the writing.

❖ Allow your child to feel ownership of his or her work; to feel that the changes came primarily from him or her.

❖ Be a model for your child by writing messages, letters, and directions. Be willing to change your own work when someone says that part of it is not clear.

Your role in advancing the writing skills of your children may be viewed as that of an adult companion. You encourage your child to express his feelings and thoughts, and you respond as a friend or companion would. Talk about what you like and what you find clear. And then ask your child to explain or to provide more specific examples for those statements you do not understand. In that way, you can give your child direction without making a lot of negative comments.

Activities for Fun and Learning

If kids experience writing as a meaningful activity, they may have a more positive attitude about it in school. Select one of the following activities to do with your child.

Written Talk

Pretend you and your child are allowed to communicate only by writing letters or notes to each other—no talking is allowed. Leave notes for your child to describe activities for the day and be sure to include some questions that she can respond to by sending you a note.

Make Books

If there is a workshop at your school or in your community on how to make books, be sure to sign up and attend. If not, then get a book from the library which has instructions for making books. Have your child draw pictures for his story first and then write the text under each picture. After the story is complete, compile it into book form and have your child design the cover. Finally, be sure to have him autograph the title page

Guided Fantasy

This activity helps children to use their creative minds to make up an imaginary story. First, have your child close her eyes; then, you will describe an imaginary

journey in a calm voice. After you have completed the trip, have your child describe what she saw and how the trip ended. Then, if your child wishes, she could write down the story or create an imaginary journey for you to listen to and complete. The following are examples of a fantasy experience that you might use:

Sensory-Awareness Statement
Close your eyes and relax in your chair . . . Now listen to the noises in the room . . . Can you hear them? Feel the temperature of the room . . . Is it hot or cold?

Setting Statement
Now turn the sounds of this room into the sounds of the meadow . . . Listen to the sounds of the meadow . . . What kind of day is it? . . . Sunny? . . . Cloudy? . . . Hot? . . . Cold? . . . Imagine that you are walking on a narrow pathway toward a mountain.

Calming Statement
A calm breeze is blowing gently on you as you walk down . . . down . . . down a pathway . . . With each step the mountain comes closer . . . and closer . . . and closer.

Action Statement and Calming Statement
As you reach the mountain you begin to climb up . . .
up . . . up and around and around the side of the
mountain . . . Through the clouds . . . you climb
up . . . up . . . up.

This activity was taken from Dorothy J. Watson's
*Ideas and Insights: Language Arts in the Elementary
School.*

Author Signing
Visit a library or bookstore when an author of children's
books will be signing copies of her books. Talk to your
child about the author before going and have your
child think of a question that he might like to ask the
author. This activity allows your child to meet a "real"
writer and to become more enthusiastic about improving his own writing skills.

Another Viewpoint
Upside Down Tales is a series that presents a traditional
tale and then the same story from another character's
point of view. Look for one of the following titles:

Little Red Riding Hood: The Wolf's Tale, by Della
    Rowland
Hansel and Gretel: The Witch's Story, by Sheila Black
Jack and the Beanstalk: The Beanstalk Incident, by
    Tim Paulson
Cinderella: Cinderella: The Untold Story, by Russell
    Shorto
Then read one of the books and rewrite the story
from another character's perspective or give your
opinion about what really happened in the story.

Books for Parents

You Can Help Your Young Child with Writing, by Marcia Baghban. Suggests methods parents can use to help develop their children's writing at home. Offers writing and reading activities.

Beginning Literacy and Your Child, by Steven B. and Linda R. Silvern. Recommends ways parents can participate in the development of their children's literacy. Provides activities for talking, reading, writing, and listening.

Creating Readers and Writers, by Nancy L. Roser. Provides suggestions to help parents encourage their children to read. Offers several practical activities for parents.

101 Ideas to Help Your Child Learn to Read and Write, by Mary and Richard Behm. Offers 101 practical suggestions for parents to help their children develop reading and writing skills in the home environment. Ideas include bedtime activities, using television, travel, games, and many other ways to incorporate literacy into the home.

Books for Parents and Children to Share

Ages 4–6

More First Words: On My Street, by Margaret Miller. Bold print words and photographs present several everyday objects a boy sees in his neighborhood. Helps a child associate a word or words with a specific object.

When You Were a Baby, by Ann Jonas. Shows, through large print and pictures, things a child can do now that she was not able to do when she was a baby. Helps a child reading this book to see her own growth and development.

A Family for Jamie: An Adoption Story, by Suzanne Bloom. Follows a young couple through the adoption process, from their expectations and planning to Jamie's arrival in their home. A warm, thoughtful story that expresses a family's love for their adopted baby.

Bigmama's, by Donald Crews. The author shares his childhood memories of summer trips to his Bigmama's house. He reminisces about visiting with family members, adventures he had, and activities on the farm.

The Way I Feel Sometimes, by Beatrice Schenk de Regniers. A collection of children's poems that convey their thoughts and emotions about their world. Lively watercolor pictures accompany the text.

Ages 6–8

Once in a Blue Moon, by Nicola Morgan. Meet Aunt Floydie and her hilarious friends and help them celebrate her birthday. Characters use idioms to express themselves, and the text is illustrated accordingly.

The Star Maiden, by Barbara Juster Esbensen; *Quillworker: A Cheyenne Legend,* by Terri Cohlene. Both books represent written forms of oral tales which were told to explain occurrences in nature. Gives children examples of expressing spoken stories in written form.

Tonight Is Carnaval, by Arthur Dorros. Illustrated with photographs of arpilleras (folk-art wall hangings). A Peruvian child explains how he and his family and friends prepare for and go to Carnaval. As he tells about life in the Andes Mountains, he gives readers a glimpse of his family's culture.

Geranium Morning, by E. Sandy Powell. Tells the story of Timothy, whose father is killed in an accident, and his friend, Frannie, whose mother dies after suffering from an incurable disease. Reveals some of the ways they both grieve and how they support each other through difficult times.

The Jolly Postman or Other People's Letters and *The Jolly Christmas Postman,* by Janet and Allan Ahlberg. Both books present various ways people communicate through writing. These delightful and imaginative collections include greeting cards, personal and business letters, advertisements, invitations, story books, a guide, and a postcard. Goldilocks, B. B. Wolf, and Cinderella are just a few of the characters sending these messages.

Ages 8–10

Danger on the African Grassland, by Elisabeth Sackett. The author has written this story about a mother rhinoceros and her offspring to communicate a message about saving endangered animals from human destruction.

All the Colors of the Race, by Arnold Adoff. Poems expressing the thoughts of a person whose heritage is both black and white, and Protestant and Jewish. Provides a message of hope for the future.

Song of the Trees, by Mildred D. Taylor. Based on a true story that occurred in rural Mississippi during the Depression. The author recounts her father's description of the huge trees on their homestead and his family's struggle to save them. A touching story depicting a love of nature and a fight for personal integrity.

Chingis Khan, by Demi. Based on both history and legend, this tale portrays the life of a boy, Temujin, who later became the infamous Chingis Khan. Parents may point out to their children that people who wrote historical accounts have affected the way we perceive history now, because of the way they expressed themselves and their opinions in their writings.

My Life (and nobody else's), by Delia Ephron and Lorraine Bodger. Bold and flashy graphics illustrate this fill-in-the-blanks type of diary for recording thoughts, feelings, and facts about a child's life. Pages include space for writing about school, family, friends, emotions, music, problems, pets, dreams, and rules.

Kids Explore America's Hispanic Heritage, by the Westridge Young Writers Workshop. Written for kids, by kids, to give readers a view of America's Hispanic culture. Covers history, food, festivals, art, stories, and language. This book was developed by students in the Westridge Young Writers Workshop, Jefferson County, Colorado. Provides an example of children writing for a purpose.

Appreciating
Poetry

$\mathbf{A}$ recent popular song had these words toward the end:

> "Did you ever know that you're my hero,
> and everything I would like to be?
> I can fly higher than an eagle,
> 'cause you are the wind beneath my wings."

When we sing a song, the words seem to come easily, without thought. We feel the emotion partly because of the music and partly because the lyrics fill our imaginations with images—"hero," "fly like an eagle," "wind beneath my wings." That's poetry.

Usually we don't think of a song as poetry, do we? We think of it as music because it sets a beat in our brain. But those words and images that stimulate our feelings are the things of which poetry is made. Do you remember this?

> Hickory, dickory, dock.
> The mouse ran up the clock.
> The clock struck one.
> The mouse ran down.
> Hickory, dickory, dock.

That's one of the nursery rhymes I remember from my childhood. I hope it was part of your childhood, too. Nursery rhymes are also poetry. Often with bizarre images and rhythm and rhyme, nursery rhymes tickle the fancy of young children who love to repeat the rhythmic phrases and probably smile over the strange images that these rhymes bring forth:

Jack fell down and broke his crown.
And Jill came tumbling after.

or

Hey diddle diddle, the cat and the fiddle.
The cow jumped over the moon.
The little dog laughed to see such sport.
And the dish ran away with the spoon.

That's the way poetry starts for most of us—in nursery rhymes and in popular songs. We love those forms of poetry. But what happens to change our minds? Why do many of us begin to think poetry is not for us? Perhaps we let the study of poetry in school distract us from the fun, the uplifting feelings, and the pleasure we got from playing with language through poetry when we were very young.

The study of poetry might have seemed more sophisticated and aloof than we wanted to be. So we pushed the word poetry into a category with words like philosophy, literary symbolism, and other words that college professors like to talk about. As a result, we may deprive our children of the fun, the rhythm, and the learning that can take place through poetry.

Yes, learning not only takes place through poetry, but poetry also makes it easier to learn, which is better than trying to force-feed the information into our minds. Do you remember this?

One little, two little, three little Indians.
Four little, five little, six little Indians.
Seven little, eight little, nine little Indians.
Ten little Indian boys.

What are children learning with that short song, with that rhythmic poem? That's right. It's a counting poem. In a similar way, we teach the ABC's with the "Alphabet Song," and we teach the fifty states with the "Fifty Nifty States" song. Songs and jingles give us many opportunities to ask questions and to help our children think. For example:

> Twinkle, twinkle, little star.
> How I wonder what you are.

You see, there is a question raised in the poem. Without dwelling on it, we can ask aloud: "Do you ever wonder what a star is?" And so we open the window to our child's curiosity—even if no specific answer is offered.

As parents, we can take our cue from the songs and jingles that we use to teach young children. By using them, we allow the child's fascination with rhythm and her natural curiosity about language to take over. In other words, we don't have to quiz our children after reciting or singing a poem. We don't have to pressure them to memorize a poem. If it is worth its salt, they will recite and play with the poem again and again—just as we sing a song again and again when it expresses a feeling that is important to us.

Promoting Poetry

If poetry expresses feelings better than most other forms of communication, and if poetry tends to make us curious about language, then we need to look for ways to make poetry a part of our consciousness more often than we do. For example, why not read a poem every day—at least for yourself—and also for your children. There are poetry books for all occasions, and your librarian would be happy to loan one to you. Read one to start the day; read one to end the day; read one when you are sad; read one when you are glad. There are recommended books of poetry in the books section of this chapter.

Sometimes your child will doubt his or her attractiveness; everyone does at various times in their lives. Then you can remind your child of the time when the wicked Queen in Snow White says:

> Mirror, mirror, on the wall,
> Who's the fairest of them all?

Or you could go to the index of a poetry book and look for a poem called "The Mirror" by Robert Graves.

> "Mirror mirror tell me
> Am I pretty or plain?
> Or am I downright ugly,
> And ugly to remain?"

"Shall I marry a gentleman?
Shall I marry a clown?
Or shall I marry
Old Knives and Scissors
Shouting through the town?"

The reference to "old knives and scissors" may cause your child to ask what that means. And you can explain that in days gone by, some people roamed the streets of the town selling old knives and scissors or sharpening knives and scissors. They would stand in the streets and shout about their business. It was a hard life, and not one that most people would choose.

Another good way to stimulate your child's interest in poetry is by writing poetry. I don't mean you have to write poems, but you may do so. What may be more manageable is for you and your child to illustrate a poem and turn it into a small book. All you have to do is take a line or two from a poem, write it on a page, and then draw a picture or cut out a picture that represents your image of those lines. For example, Stevie Smith has a poem entitled "The Frog Prince" which begins with four lines that could easily take two pages with illustration:

Page one with an illustration: "I am a frog
   I live under a spell"
Page two: "I live at the bottom
   Of a green well."

Or think about how you could illustrate William Wordsworth's well-known poem, "The Daffodils," which begins:

"I wandered lonely as a cloud
That floats on high o'er vales and hills,
When all at once I saw a crowd,
A host of golden daffodils

Beside the lake, beneath the trees,
Fluttering and dancing in the breeze."

Your child could make a little greeting card booklet out of that poem and send it to Grandma and Grandpa.

In all that you do to promote poetry with your children, please remember that poetry stimulates feelings that may make their ears twitch and their eyes pop. It should start their tongue working over words and their feet tapping, tapping out the dance of language and life.

Parents' Questions about Poetry

We would like to reply to a few questions parents frequently ask concerning children and poetry.

❖ How can I get my older children interested in reading poetry at home?

As a parent, I think one of the best suggestions I ever received for making poetry part of our reading was the advice of one poet, "Keep a poem in your pocket." Now I didn't really do this, but I did get the idea of keeping a poem handy or close by. When I come across a poem that I enjoy and think my children might enjoy, I place it in a notebook for family sharing.

Why don't you show your children that you are interested in poetry by what you do? Start collecting your favorite poems. Have a poem ready for every mood, for every occasion: a poem to pull out on a rainy day when there can be no outdoor play or a poem to read when someone is feeling sad or discouraged. For example, Robert Louis Stevenson's "Happy Thought":

"The world is so full of a number of things,
I'm sure we should all be as happy as kings."

Introducing poetry means knowing where to find poems your children can enjoy and introducing them at opportune times.

Start a notebook or a card file of favorite poems. If you group the poems by subject or mood—pets, birthdays, celebrations, love, and so on—you and your children will be able to make selections quickly. Perhaps your children will offer you their own choices. Maybe they will want to start their own notebooks of favorite poems.

Make a habit of reading poetry to your children during the day—a funny poem, a touching poem, story poems, singing poems. Invite your children to select a poem to read aloud each day. Place the poem on the

table or on the counter, post it on the refrigerator, or leave it in a prominent place where they can reread it easily.

❖ My son has reading problems. Would poetry be too difficult for him to read?

Poems can help children develop reading fluency. Select poems that are fun to read and that will keep your son's interest. Some poems have built-in rhythm that makes them more memorable and rememberable. It's unlikely that your son will remember whole paragraphs of a story, but he can learn many lines of poems and songs that are entertaining. The rhythmic sounds and patterns make poems perfect for chanting. This helps your son read them because the patterns of poetic language are predictable enough for your son to keep on reading.

You might try reading together with your son. You can be the model for reading the poem while your son repeats what you have read.

For example, by the time you are at one of the last verses in "The House that Jack Built," your son may be able to recite the last few lines with you.

> This is the maiden all forlorn,
> That milked the cow with the crumpled horn,
> That tossed the dog,
> That worried the cat,
> That killed the rat,
> That ate the malt,
> That lay in the house that Jack built.

❷ **Sometimes my daughter must write a poem for homework. We both feel very frustrated with this type of assignment. How can I help her write poems?**

In order for children to be able to write poems, they must read poems. As you read poetry with your daughter, comment upon certain words that are especially interesting, exciting, or unusual. Choose short poems that have humor and those that use words in a playful, fun way. For example,

> Hoddley, poddley, puddle and fogs,
> Cats are to marry the poodle dogs;
> Cats in blue jackets and dogs in red hats,
> What will become of the mice and the rats?

Once your daughter has listened to or read this kind of poetry, she may have a sense of how poems flow and rhyme. Children often get caught up in trying to make the words rhyme and are unable to move forward with their writing. Provide examples of poems that rhyme and poems that don't rhyme so that your

daughter knows the difference, like William Blake's "The Divine Image." Here is one of the verses:

"For Mercy has a human heart;
Pity, a human face;
And Love, the human form divine;
And Peace, the human dress."

As you begin to help your daughter write poems, have her concentrate on the five senses. You might begin with a timely experience. Seasonal themes work well. You might say, "Close your eyes. It's Spring. What do you see? What do you hear? Let your senses explore. What do you smell, taste, feel?" Or you might take a Fall walk, talk about colors or the movement of leaves, and talk about words that can describe your feelings and thoughts. Smell a leaf—it smells musty, peppery. Feel a leaf—it feels crumbly, dry.

Talk about what she might say in her poem. If your child seems to be groping for a word, give her some choices. You might say, "The leaves fall down. . . can you use another word that helps me see how they fall?" If she is still blocked, ask: "Did they float, drift, whisper?" Let her choose a word, thus giving her responsibility of choice and ownership. Often, she will then produce her own word. In considering choices of poetic words, your daughter is building a reservoir of rich language, with you acting as a resource.

Activities for Fun and Learning

Have some fun with poetry by trying one or two of the following activities you and your child can do together.

Play On!

Listening to nursery rhymes can be a fun way to introduce young children to the rhyme and rhythm of language. Try playing a tape or record of nursery rhymes for your child to listen to instead of watching television.

Oh Nonsense!

Edward Lear wrote many nonsense poems. The following is one of his verses:

"There was an Old Man
of the Isles,
Whose face was pervaded with
smiles;
He sang 'High dum diddle,'
And played on the fiddle,
That amiable Man of the Isles."

Together, substitute your own character and use Mr. Lear's pattern to make a similar nonsense poem. For example:

There was a Young Person of Nor,
Who fished too far from the shore;
A strong gust blew,
And away she flew,
That flighty Young Person of Nor.

Give Me Five

Cinquain is a form of poetry developed by Adelaide Crapsey. It consists of five lines with two syllables in the first line, four in the second, six in the third, eight in the fourth, and two in the fifth. These lines are written without the use of rhyme. For example:

Cold pop,
Tickles my nose.
As it slides down my throat,
Hear it bubble, gurgle, fizzle.
Sip fun.

Books for Parents

Poem-making: Ways to Begin Writing Poetry, by Myra Cohn Livingston . Introduces the mechanics of writing poetry. Covers different voices of poetry, types of rhyme and other elements of sound including rhythm and metrics. Discusses various forms of poetry and figures of speech.

Finger Rhymes, collected and illustrated by Marc Brown. Includes traditional and less-familiar rhymes. Easy-to-follow diagrams show finger gestures to go along with each rhyme.

The Healing Power of Poetry, by Dr. Smiley Blanton. Shares how to use poetry to help ease and cope with anxiety, loneliness, anger, depression, and frustration.

Books for Parents and Children to Share

Ages 4–6

A Fine Fat Pig, by Mary Ann Hoberman. Contains fourteen animal poems with bright, bold pictures. The artist painted the pictures and the author wrote the poems to go along with the paintings.

The Sunday Tree, by Eloise Greenfield. Includes lively illustrations and expressive verse that portray life in the Bahamas. Poems symbolize people, animals, and settings.

Bungalow Fungalow, by Pegi Deitz Shea. Depicts Billy's stay at his grandparents' bungalow on the beach. Begins with the invitation to visit and concludes with the trip back home.

Pudding and Pie, chosen by Sarah Williams. Contains forty traditional nursery rhymes including "Jack and Jill," "Little Tommy Tucker," "Hey, Diddle, Diddle," "Old King Cole," and "Little Miss Muffet."

All Join In, by Quentin Blake. Six lively poems invite the reader to join in the fun and excitement that can be found in daily life. Shows children enjoying singing, sliding, and even cleaning.

Rain, Rain, Go Away! A Book of Nursery Rhymes, illustrated by Jonathan Langley. Offers a large collection of nursery rhymes. Delightful illustrations accompany the text.

Ages 6–8

Up in the Mountains and Other Poems of Long Ago, by Claudia Lewis. Recounts a young girl's childhood during the turn of the century in America. Sketches are in black and white.

Side by Side: Poems to Read Together, collected by Lee Bennett Hopkins. Contains poems by Lewis Carroll, Robert Frost, Aileen Fisher, Eve Merriam, and others. Bright and lively illustrations accompany the text. These poems have been selected specifically for sharing.

The Nonsense Poems of Edward Lear, illustrated by Leslie Brooke. A collection of foolish, laughable, and ridiculous poems by the English humorist and artist, Edward Lear.

Scary Poems for Rotten Kids, by Sean O'Huigin. Poems focus on "the monstrous episodes in the life of any ordinary child." Full of creepy, scary, and weird things.

Bear in Mind: A Book of Bear Poems, selected by Bobbye S. Goldstein. Presents through poetry, polar bears, honey bears, circus bears, zoo bears, teddy bears, and even a grandpa bear.

A Child's Treasury of Seaside Verse, complied by Mark Daniel. This collection is a medley of poems about the sea, and is written by some of the best American and English writers. Paintings and engravings from the Victorian and Edwardian eras illustrate the text.

Ages 8–10

Rhymes and Verses: Collected Poems for Young People, by Walter de la Mare. Includes over three hundred poems covering a wide variety of subject matter.

For Laughing Out Loud: Poems to Tickle Your Funny Bone, selected by Jack Prelutsky. A collection of

132 hilarious poems, "and if you almost split your sides, that's what this book is for."

Handspan of the Red Earth: An Anthology of American Farm Poems, edited by Catherine Lewallen Marconi. Contains an assortment of contemporary poetry about farming the diverse and unique lands of America. Includes poems by Galway Kinnell, Mary Swander, Dennis Schmitz, Maxine Kumin, and many others.

Roald Dahl's Revolting Rhymes, Roald Dahl. Offers unique retellings of the following fairy tales: "Cinderella," "Snow White and the Seven Dwarfs," "Jack and the Beanstalk," "Goldilocks and the Three Bears," "Little Red Riding Hood," and "The Three Little Pigs."

You Come Too: Favorite Poems for Young Readers, by Robert Frost. Contains a selection of poems by the Pulitzer prize winning poet, Robert Frost. Shares thoughts from his heart.

The Usborne Book of Funny Poems, selected by Heather Amery. This assortment of poetry consists of whimsical new poems for children. Colorful and amusing pictures accompany the text.

Where the Sidewalk Ends and *A Light in the Attic,* by Shel Silverstein. These collections of poems and drawings are favorites of every age group.

Enjoying Art All around Us

Have you noticed how often children today bring home drawings or craft projects from school? Teachers often ask children to express their feelings about a story by drawing a picture or by making a collage.

Have you noticed the art in children's books? What dramatic displays of color and imagination!

Have you noticed that even school textbooks look more like well-illustrated library books than like the grayish textbooks of the past? If you look at your children's reading textbooks, for example, you will probably find chapters on famous artists or famous museums with color photographs of their well-known paintings and sculptures.

These examples of illustrations in books, and the use of art as a means to respond to stories or to science lessons, show the value we place on visual images. Works of beauty and imagination can uplift us, excite us, give us joy, and tell us important things about our humanity. We all know that children love to express themselves through arts and crafts activities. With simple materials like crayons, paper, yarn, and glue, young children will create their impression of the warmth of sunshine or the feeling of raindrops on their heads. By encouraging our children to describe and interpret their art work for us, we give them an opportunity to tell us about their feelings, about their humanity.

One of the ways that you can stimulate your child's interest in art is to make him or her a craft cabinet out of four or five shoe boxes that are pasted together like a mini-display case. Each compartment can hold separate materials—pieces of cloth, crayons, bits of styrofoam, leaves and twigs, colored paper, and so on. In this craft cabinet your child can store the small treasures that can be used to create impressions or to tell stories. After reading a book together, for instance, you might ask your child to make a picture that describes his feelings about the story.

Older children, too, may want to use art as a way to respond to the books they read. One of my daughters, while in middle school, drew a watercolor of a sad-faced Vietnamese girl. This was her response to a story about boat people who braved the dangers of the sea in order to find a better life. I framed that picture and hung it on my wall. It is still there many years after it was first drawn because it shows my daughter's concern for other people.

Displaying your child's drawings, paintings, and sculpture is a way of encouraging his creativity and of showing your pleasure with these artistic forms of expression. Many parents use the refrigerator as a bulletin board for their children's art. You may want to use your child's art as a kind of postcard to grandparents or other relatives. Just as words can communicate and can indicate child development, so can art.

Trees and Museums

We don't want to give the impression that the only way to participate in art is to draw or to sculpt something. When you and your child take a walk, notice variations in colors, feel the bark of trees to sense their texture, admire the shape of a building, or feel the serenity of water in a pond, you are sensing art. Your child will grow artistically from those experiences.

When you visit art fairs or museums and comment briefly on what you like and what you do not like, you are fostering appreciation for artistic expression. Children don't want lengthy lectures, just a brief comment on your preferences. These easy, natural steps into the world of art have the same effect that reading stories do. They build awareness and appreciation through exposure.

Artists express their ideas and their feelings through color and shape and texture. Their ideas and feelings may lift our spirits or may make us angry, just as words in a book may do. We praise or reject ideas in books, and we do the same thing with works of art. In fact, that's a valuable lesson for our children to learn—that art can stimulate critical thinking. Our thoughts about art usually begin with an overall reaction, for example, "I really like that painting," or "I wouldn't want that thing in my house." Then we start to figure out why we like or dislike it so much. By analyzing our reactions out loud, we show our children that it's okay to think differently about art depending on the criteria that we apply.

Your children's school fosters art appreciation through stories and illustrations in textbooks and through museum visits and discussions about various kinds of art. Almost all reading textbooks for elementary school children have stories about artists and their work. Full-color illustrations of famous paintings or sculptures accompany these stories. Similarly, many library books offer the same broad opportunities for children to see and to discuss art and artists. Through books, through visits to museums, and by looking at the art that people display in their homes and in their businesses, your children can decide gradually what they like and why. They can decide whether they want art to brighten and beautify their lives or to jar them into thinking seriously about life—or both.

What Parents Can Do

When you hang a picture of Mickey Mouse in your child's bedroom, you are starting your child's art education. That picture says that art brightens our lives and reminds us to smile, even when it is raining. When you hang a mobile over your child's crib, you are doing more than giving her something to watch as it moves and swings in the air. You are enabling her to understand that art may be three dimensional. When you display a photograph on your table, you inform your child that art can also show real people and events. That doesn't mean that every photograph is artistic, but the presence of photographs along with other kinds of illustrations and figurines sends a message to your child—various kinds of art fill our lives. If your children produce something that you feel deserves special recognition, frame it. Then it takes its place beside other pictures that you have framed and displayed.

In our house, we have a gallery of our children's art. The hallway to the bedrooms displays the special pieces that each of our four children have produced. Some are drawings, some are collages, some are poems that are illustrated with snapshots of members of our family. Each in its own way represents the talents of its creator and indicates the strong feelings that went into its creation. Not that these pieces have great value outside our family; rather, they make a statement that says we value the imaginative work of the people who live in this house.

Here are a few things that you may want to try to develop your children's appreciation of art:

❖ Show your own enthusiasm for art and encourage your children to catch your excitement.

❖ Take a walk in your neighborhood and look at building design. Talk about the shapes used, location and size of windows and doors, and decorative elements in the structure. Imagine how the building would look if you changed one design element. Talk about how the design relates to the building's function.

❖ Provide materials and a place where your children can explore different kinds of art. Use an old table with a drawer—or that cabinet made of shoe boxes—for crayons, paint, paper, buttons, yarn, and other materials that can serve young artists.

❖ Praise your children's efforts. Try asking your children to tell you about what they have made. Children may have a story to tell about their creations. By listening to their explanations, you will know what to praise in their work.

❖ When you visit craft shows or museums, grab your children's attention by saying they will see old jewelry, or good luck charms, or art that was buried with a mummy.

❖ Get a variety of picture books from the library or your bookstore, and talk about the styles of art, the colors used, and how the illustrations affect your impression of the story being told.

❖ See if your child wants to write and illustrate a story—perhaps a fictional story or an account of some event in your child's life. Glue or sew the pages together, and your child is an author!

❖ Use building blocks or graph paper as a way of planning a home and the various rooms in it. This is a way for children to build their own castles.

❖ Photography is an exciting way for most children to express themselves. This hobby isn't that expensive any more since you can buy disposable or plastic cameras at your local discount stores. Encourage experimentation by using different angles and playing with lights and shadows. Books on photography will help children think of ways of creating special photo albums or displays.

A Final Word on Art

We as parents can have an important influence on the way our children appreciate and create art. Through art we can express our perceptions of the world—its sorrows and its joys. Art helps each of us learn about life and about our own feelings. You can work with other parents to improve the role of art education in your children's school, and you can certainly make your home a place that reminds your children that art stimulates their thinking and improves their lives.

Activities for Fun and Learning

There are many ways to enjoy and share art with children. Select one of the following activities for you and your child to do together.

Read and Sketch

After reading a story, encourage your child to think about what he read and then draw a sketch of "what the selection meant to him, or what he made of the reading." Draw a sketch yourself, and then talk about why you both have different pictures/interpretations. Share with your child that drawing is a way to express his thoughts. Tell him there won't be a right or wrong sketch.

Get the Picture

Gather several books that demonstrate different methods of illustration. Together, compare and contrast the media and technique used by various artists. Discuss the role illustrations play in telling the stories. Here are some examples you can use:

Manatee on Location, by Kathy Darling. Photographs by Tara Darling.

Rain Player, by David Wisniewski. Cut-paper illustrations.

A Wave in Her Pocket: Stories from Trinidad, by Lynn Joseph. Scratchboard illustrations by Brian Pinkney.

The Journey of Meng, by Doreen Rappaport. Watercolor illustrations by Yang Ming-Yi.

The Enchanted Wood, by Ruth Sanderson. Illustrated with oil paintings.

Tour d'Art

If you do not have a gallery in your local area, or if a particular museum you are interested in is too far away, find out what resources are available at your library. Most libraries have books and videos that pre-sent museums and art from around the world.

Books for Parents

Let's Learn about Arts and Crafts, by Gaye Ruschen. Presents art activities which enhance children's visual perception, vocabulary, listening skills, self-concept, and decision making abilities. Covers drawing, coloring, cutting, pasting, painting, and creating collages. Includes several reproducible patterns.

Mudworks: Creative Clay, Dough, and Modeling Experiences, by MaryAnn F. Kohl. Suggests over 100 art activities to promote children's creativity, motor development, and visual perception. Offers ideas to use with playdough, bread dough, papier-mache, edible art dough, modeling mixtures, and plaster of Paris.

A Viewer's Guide to Art: A Glossary of Gods, People, and Creatures, by Marvin S. Shaw and Richard Warren. This concise handbook identifies and describes mythological, religious, and historical figures, creatures, and symbols found in art. Serves as a source to enhance the art viewer's understanding and appreciation of art and artists.

The *Key to Art* series:
> *The Key to Painting*
> *The Key to Gothic Art*
> *The Key to Renaissance Art*
> *The Key to Baroque Art*
> *The Key to Art from Romanticism to*
> *Impressionism*
> *The Key to Modern Art of the Early 20th Century*
> Introduces the world of art in a brief, readable format. Includes full-color reproductions as well as information on both artists and artwork. This series gives an overview of the historical development of art from the Gothic period to the early 20th century.

Books for Parents and Children to Share

Ages 4–6

Babson's Bestiary, by Jane F. Babson. Presents the alphabet through unique illustrations created using a variety of media and formats. Each page displays a letter, a creature whose name begins with that letter, and a rhyming verse about the creature. Enables kids to learn their alphabet and view different types of art at the same time.

Straight Is a Line: A Book about Lines, by Sharon Lerner. Uses familiar objects to demonstrate different types of lines. Brief text and bold graphics illustrate lines that are straight, parallel, vertical, and horizontal, as well as lines that curve, arc, and zigzag. Children can match the lines shown with lines they see all around them.

I Want a Blue Banana! by Joyce and James Dunbar. Dan accompanies his mother to the grocery store, and while she is looking for her lost list in the produce section, he learns the names of several colors and fruits. Displays various colors found in nature through an amusing shopping adventure.

Rummage Sale: A Fun Book of Shapes and Colors, by Neil Morris. Katie is selling a variety of objects at her school's rummage sale. As customers come by Katie's table, readers can determine which item each person buys. Presents an opportunity for children to describe different shapes and colors they see on Katie's table.

A Potter, by Douglas Florian. Large print, sparse text, and full-page pictures explain, step by step, how an artist creates a piece of pottery out of a lump of clay. Gives children an inside view of an artist at work.

Ed Emberley's Drawing Book: Make a World, by Ed Emberley. Details step-by-step procedures for drawing a variety of objects, including: vehicles, animals, people, buildings, furniture, plants, and other miscellaneous items.

Ages 6–8

Gerald-Not-Practical, by Helena Clare Pittman. Gerald loves to draw, but his family wishes he would do something more practical. Gerald eventually teaches his family that drawing makes him happy, and shows them how important it is to do something you truly love, even if others don't think it is practical. Supports children who enjoy art more than other activities.

A Visit to the Art Galaxy, by Annie Reiner. Peter and Bess are taken to an art museum by their mother. While peering into a painting, they mysteriously visit several artists including Matisse, Picasso, Rothko, and others. Uses an intriguing narrative form to give children an introduction to modern and contemporary art.

Bonjour, Mr. Satie, by Tomie dePaola. When Pablo and Henri present their new paintings at Gertrude's Salon, terrible arguments begin. Mr. Satie, a traveling cat, is chosen to judge whose paintings are the best. All of Paris waits as Mr. Satie makes his decision. Parents can use this book to introduce children to Pablo Picasso and Henri Matisse and compare their work.

Cherries and Cherry Pits, by Vera B. Williams. Bidemmi draws lots and lots of pictures, and with each picture she tells a story while she draws. Demonstrates the creative outlet art provides for children and the value of a good imagination.

Getting to Know the World's Greatest Artists series, written by Mike Venezia. Each book features an individual artist, including: Rembrandt, Picasso, Botticelli, Cassatt, Van Gogh, Goya, Hopper, and Monet. The author believes, if kids can look at art in a fun way, and think of artists as real people, the exciting world of art will be open to them for the rest of their lives.

The Art Lesson, by Tomie dePaola. The author shares his love of art by telling a story about his first-grade art class. He learns how to cooperate in class and still express his own individuality and creativity.

Ages 8–10

The Young Artist, by Thomas Locker. Full-page illustrations by the highly acclaimed artist Thomas Locker recount the story of a young artist, Adrian Van der Weld. Adrian faces the dilemma of painting the king's courtiers as they want to look, not as they truly appear. Even though it is difficult and dangerous, Adrian maintains his sense of integrity and receives his just reward.

Rembrandt's Beret, by Johnny Alcorn. Tiberius becomes lost while waiting for a rainstorm to end, and discovers the "Hall of the Old Masters." Mysteriously, he meets the artists, and Rembrandt paints a portrait of Tiberius during his stay. Introduces some of the Old Masters, including Michelangelo, Rubens, Raphael, Titian, and Rembrandt in fantasy format.

The Collage Book, by Hannah Tofts. Explains what a collage is and gives simple instructions on how to make one. Presents examples of collages made from paper, fabric, wood, food, photos, and several other objects.

Come Look with Me: Enjoying Art with Children and *Come Look with Me: Exploring Landscape Art with Children,* by Gladys S. Blizzard. Each book consists of full-color reproductions, brief biographies of artists and open-ended questions to promote discussion and critical thinking. Provides a unique and enjoyable way to enhance art appreciation at home.

The World of Art, through the Eyes of Artists, by Wendy and Jack Richardson. Titles in the series include the following: Animals, Cities, Entertainers, Families, The Natural World, and Water. Each book presents illustrations of art which deal with a specific topic. Includes specific information about both the artist and the accompanying work.

Creative Expression through Music and Dance

A song may have saved the life of Jessica McClure. She's the little girl from Texas who made national headlines when she fell down an old well and was trapped there for almost three days. For all that time the little girl was wedged in a narrow, cold, abandoned well.

As workers tried frantically to rescue her, they heard Jessica singing to herself, over and over again, as though she was singing a chant for life. Someone had taught her a song—a song that may have saved her life. No one thought that her bruised, hungry body could withstand the underground cold. They were afraid that she would die of hypothermia. But she didn't. She kept singing that song.

Sometimes we think of music as merely entertainment, but it is much more than that. Music operates like an instinctual language. Basic rhythms calm or excite our nervous systems. That's why we can't help tapping our feet to rap music and to marches. Certain sounds and certain tempos can make us feel sad or happy. Music captures our attention and enables us to recall long-forgotten memories.

Film makers and TV producers are aware of the power of music over our bodies and minds, and use it to elicit moods and feelings. Doctors and dentists often use music to help their patients relax, and producers of sports events use it to increase the excitement of games. In a similar way, teachers and parents can use music for learning. If children's nervous systems are keyed up, some teachers will play march music while students march around the room for a few minutes to ease some of their tension. Then they will play soft relaxing music to help children concentrate on their desk work. Parents, of course, have always sung lullabies to calm their children, especially when they want them to go to sleep.

Teachers and parents have found that music makes it easier to remember things, such as the alphabet through the "ABC song." Chants, songs, and rap music are used to remember everything from multiplication tables to state capitals. Dancing and hand-clapping can be used in a similar fashion. Young children can use their bodies to form the shapes of the alphabet so as to learn and to remember them. Older children can use choral music to improve pronunciation and to remember poetry.

Art and Fun

We don't want to give the impression that you need to use music and dance primarily to improve memory or to calm the nervous system for study in school. Music and dance are related art forms that help people express their emotions and develop a sense of beauty or power, as well as their natural abilities. You can help your children to explore the arts by buying, or helping them make, simple instruments, such as hand drums, triangles, rhythm sticks, or tambourines—anything they can shake, bang, or clink. Children can also use a tape recorder, which will give them a chance to play tapes or to record their own songs, thus improving their sense of music and dance.

All you have to do is watch young children dancing or imitating a musician to know that they have a great time using music to stimulate their imaginations. You can use this sense of fun and involvement to help them become curious about the musical expression of moods, sounds in nature (a storm, for example), and how different instruments can represent body movements (the flute for skipping, the trombone for marching, the violin for swaying, and so on). You might ask your children to assign a color to certain instruments as they listen to them in a band or orchestra. The guitar might sound green, the trumpet red, and the bass brown. It doesn't matter how they associate colors with the music they hear. You are simply trying to help them appreciate music through all their senses, not just hearing. These exercises will help open their imaginations to different ways of making music and dance a part of their lives.

Have you ever thought of using song books as read-along books? Many song books for children are beautifully illustrated and make wonderful read-along, sing-along books. Some have accompanying tape recordings so you and your child can learn the songs together—providing that you know the songs and are able to guide the singing. By using tape recorders, children can do their own read-sing-dance-along activities at a very early age.

Singing and dancing are a part of early childhood activities in many families—rocking with "Rock-a-Bye-Baby," playing "Patty-Cake," skipping to "Ring-around-the-Rosie." These joyful experiences shouldn't stop when a child goes to school. Through such early music and dance games, you can set the stage for long-term family fun and learning. Song books, charades, making up new verses to old songs, interpreting music through dance, selecting music for cleaning the house or eating dinner, may open your children's senses and help them to learn and to appreciate life through music and dance.

Questions about Music and Dance

Oftentimes parents are interested in involving their children in music activities or dance but have questions about it. We would like to answer some of those questions.

❖ **Our daughter is in the elementary school band and must practice at home. Her practicing can sometimes be annoying, and is just one more thing we have to work into our schedule. Do you have any suggestions for making this a pleasant experience for all of us?**

When your daughter learns a musical instrument, she must study—or practice that instrument just as she studies math, social studies, or other subjects in school. But just as others in the family must understand that her practicing is important, so too, your daughter needs to respect their right for quiet during certain times.

If possible, find a quiet place for your daughter to practice. A room away from others allows her to practice without interruptions, and she does not disturb those who are trying to concentrate on their homework or other tasks. If the sound of her practicing cannot be isolated, it might be good to select a time when other members of your family are away or doing things that do not require a great deal of concentration.

Encourage your daughter to play pieces she is good at, as well as ones on which she needs more practice. This will make everyone feel better and will give you opportunities to praise your daughter's efforts. She will need your daily encouragement for studying music, just as she needs it for reading and writing. Playing a variety of music can help motivate practice. You may want to ask her teacher to recommend sheet music that will be fun for her to play, as well as the pieces she must practice for school performances.

When your daughter has mastered a piece of music, have her play it for the family. Let everyone enjoy the results of her practicing.

❷ I heard a teacher say that music helps children learn to read. What does music have to do with reading?

Music and reading go together because singing and reading are celebrations of language. Children love to play with the words and rhythms in songs and find reflections of those rhythms and melodies in print.

Music is a natural extension of children's language and experience. Children sing songs that they hear, and are eager to see the words in print. The easiest language for them to read is that with which they are familiar and comfortable. In class they show excitement when they see the songs they know in print. Children develop a sight vocabulary and a deeper understanding of meaning as they point to words or phrases while singing along.

Songs engage children in activities that help comprehension. Using movement with songs is a wonderful way to extend comprehension. When children do the movements to "I'm a Little Tea Pot" we know that they truly have comprehended that song. Acting out a song builds bridges between reading and movement, and reading and drama. Because of their natural affinity for music, children are willing to act out songs over and over again, thus reinforcing the language and ideas in the lyrics.

❖ Why is my kindergarten son dancing in class? Aren't there more important things they should be learning?

The kind of dance that most young children do in early childhood classrooms is called "creative dance" or "creative movement." Through such creative movement to music, children explore sound and the abilities of their bodies. Their movements reflect what the music means or feels like to them. And this is one of the functions of dance—to express feelings and to interpret ideas, which are also functions of reading and writing.

Children need the opportunity to explore movement possibilities and to pay attention to what those movements feel like. Answering questions such as "How can you get higher when you jump?" or "How can you fall down without crashing to the floor?" or "How can you move your body to make it look like you are blowing in the wind?" can help your child's physical and mental development.

Dance helps young children learn about their bodies, space, time, energy, and the relationships among them. Children realize that they can make shapes and letters with their bodies; they can move with strength and lightness just as the wind moves. They learn that the movements they use to walk across a room, to reach for a toy, or to turn and bend to pick something up are also used in dancing. Children do not consider this dancing, but dance is made up of the same movements—walking, reaching, bending, turning.

The important link between "creative movement" and learning is a major reason why early childhood classrooms provide concrete experiences with music and dance. Dance is certainly not the only kind of movement young children want or need. But its emphasis on sound, rhythm, and meaning can help children understand themselves and their world.

Activities for Song and Movement

As parents, we are looking for activities that will benefit our children. Here are some music and dance activities you can enjoy with your children.

Straw Flute
Make a flute using plastic straws and masking tape. Arrange six or seven straws in a single row. Place the

tape across the outside of the straws to attach them together. Begin at the left end, skip the first straw and then cut off each straw so that it is 1/4" shorter than the one which preceded it. Gently blow across the top of the straws to create sound.

Audio-Visual Fun

Browse through the audio-visual department of your library for videos of operas, ballets, and musicals to watch with your child. Also, look for instructional videos on music or dance. Tapes, records, and CDs of all types of music are usually available to borrow. Your local library may have a special area with equipment for your listening pleasure.

Jump, Twist, and Shout

If you are not comfortable dancing with your child, try exercising to music. Jumping jacks, running or jumping in place, twists, and stretching work well.

Books for Parents

Creative Movement for the Developing Child: A Nursery School Handbook for Non-Musicians, by Clare Cherry. Recommends activities for the development of walking, running, jumping, leaping, skipping, throwing and catching movements. Also covers posture, percussion instruments, rhythmic activities, and auditory perception games.

Growing Up with Music, by Hilda Hunter. Shows parents how to make music a part of their child's life. Provides tips on musical play, games, hobbies, trips, and concerts. Discusses music enjoyment and building a home music library.

The History of Dance, by Mary Clarke and Clement Crisp. Presents the history of dance from a variety of cultures spanning more than 2,000 years. Describes different types of dance: primitive, ancient, religious, European, Eastern, social, and modern. Elaborates on the history and development of ballet.

The Music of Man, by Yehudi Menuhin and Curtis W. Davis. Explores the evolution of music from its early beginnings to the present. Outlines the social and historical development of music and its influence on humankind.

Books for Parents and Children to Share

Ages 4–6

Dance Away, by George Shannon. Rabbit loves to dance. He dances morning, noon, and night. Rabbit not only dances for fun, but helps his friends by showing them how to dance away from a hungry fox.

Obadiah Coffee and the Music Contest, by Valerie Poole. Obadiah plays like no one else, until someone puts a banana in his saxophone at the Boxwood Garden music contest. Obadiah must discover the culprit and get the contest back in full swing.

What a Noise: A Fun Book of Sounds, by Neil Morris. Sam discovers many different sounds while trying to keep things quiet around the house so his sister can take her nap. The peace and quiet ends when Sam can't stop sneezing.

Dancing, by Harriet Ziefert. Shows a group of young animals as they discover what the world of dance is all about. Includes reusable stickers with words from the story.

What Can Rabbit Hear? by Lucy Cousins. Rabbit listens to what he can hear with his big ears. Children can lift the flap on each page to reveal what rabbit hears.

The Doorknob Collection of Nursery Rhymes, by Judith Stuller Hannant. Includes "Humpty Dumpty," "This Little Piggy," "Mary Had a Little Lamb," and "Little Miss Muffet." Books have sturdy pages for easy turning.

Ages 6–8

Angelina and the Princess, by Katharine Holabird. Even though Angelina does not get the leading role in the ballet, she does her best to make the whole program successful. When the leading lady hurts her foot, Angelina steps in and saves the show.

Madame Nightingale Will Sing Tonight, by James Mayhew. The animals in the woods decide to perform an opera. Trouble arises when Madame Nightingale develops stage fright. Includes introductory information about opera.

Make Your Own Musical Instruments, by Margaret McLean. Gives instructions for making various kinds of instruments. Includes tambourine, maracas, castanets, drums, xylophone, bells, zither, and wind instruments. Covers music notation and rhythms.

I Love to Dance, by Gerry Zeck. Tony studies ballet and contemporary dance, and performs in theater groups. Describes Tony's life and his love of dancing.

Ben's Trumpet, by Rachel Isadora. Ben longs to play the trumpet, but has only an imaginary one. A musician understands Ben's yearning and helps him to realize his dream of becoming a trumpeter.

Dancing Is, by George Ancona. Describes what dancing is and explains why some people dance. Looks at dances from various parts of the world.

Ages 8–10

Mozart Tonight, by Julie Downing. Follows Mozart as he might remember his life from childhood to the performance of his opera, Don Giovanni. Also includes background information about Mozart from the author's research.

A Pianist's Debut, by Barbara Beirne. Eleven-year-old Leah attends The Juilliard School of Music in New York where she studies to become a concert pianist. Shares her love of music and growth as an artist.

The Street Dancers, by Elizabeth Starr Hill. Fitzi and her family are performers. She is busy with plays, mime acts, and commercials. Fitzi wants to find out what it is like to be a regular kid like her friends. She wants to have a normal life, but is afraid her family will never understand.

Music, by Carol Greene. A general introduction to the world of music. Covers musical language, instruments, and great composers. Also includes definitions of words from the world of music.

A Very Young Musician, by Jill Krementz. A photo essay about the life of ten-year-old Josh Broder. Josh relates his love of music and tells about learning to play the trumpet.

An Usborne Introduction: Understanding Music, by Judy Tatchell. Presents a broad range of styles and categories of music. Explores instruments, dance, voice, composition, performance, composers, and notation.

Index

Activities for fun and learning
art, 134–135
history, 69
library, 87–88
math, 48–50
poetry, 120–121
science, 30–32
writing, 100–103

Art, 127–140
activities, 134–135
books about, 136–140
motivation, 128–131
parental help, 131–134

Books for parents and children
art, 136–140
history, 70–74
library, 88–91
math, 50–54
poetry, 121–125
science, 32–35
writing, 104–107

Dance, see Music and Dance

History, 55–74
activities, 69
as exploration, 57–60
as interpretation of past events, 56
books about, 70–74
parental help, 64–68
stories, 60–63

Library, 75–91
activities, 87–88
books about, 88–91
parental help, 80–89
parents' resolutions, 80
questions about, 80–87
services for preschoolers, 77–79
services for school-age children, 79

Math, 37–54
activities, 48–50
books about, 50–54
motivation, 42–43
parental help, 42–43
problem solving, 39–42
questions about, 43–48

self-confidence, 39
skills, 40–42

Motivation
art, 128–131
history, 64–68
math, 42–43
science, 22–24
writing, 98–100

Music and Dance, 141–154
activities, 148–150
books about, 150–154
parental help, 142–145
questions about, 145–148

Parental help
art, 131–134
history, 64–68
library, 80–89
math, 42–43
music and dance,
142–145
poetry, 113–115
science, 19–45
writing, 98–100

Poetry, 109–125
activities, 120–121
books about, 121–125
parental help, 113–115
questions about, 115–120

Questions
about the library, 80–87
about math, 43–48
about music and dance,
145–148
about poetry, 115–120
about science, 24–30

Science, 19–35
activities, 30–32
books about, 32–35
flexible thinking, 21–22
motivation, 22–24
parental help, 19–24
play as a way of
approaching, 20–21
questions about, 24–30
skills, 22–24

Skills
math, 40–42
science, 22–24
writing, 99–100

Writing, 93–107
activities, 100–103
books about, 104–107
importance of personal
writing, 94–98
parental help, 98–100

Parents' Notes.

_____

_____

_____

_____

_____

_____

_____

_____

_____

_____

_____

_____

_____

_____

Parents' Notes

_____

_____

_____

_____

_____

_____

_____

_____

_____

_____

_____

_____

_____

_____

_____

From the Family Literacy Center . . .

Tapes and booklets* to accompany this book:

_____Learning Science at Home (C08; $8)
_____Learning Math at Home (C11; $8)
_____Making History Come Alive (C25; $8)
_____Using the Library (C22; $8)
_____Making Writing Meaningful (C27; $8)
_____Appreciating Poetry (C21; $8)
_____Enjoying Art All around Us (C26; $8)
_____Creative Expression through Music and Dance
        (C19; $8)

*Booklets include the information presented in this book plus
stories to read aloud or listen to with your child.

To order:
1. check off the topic(s) above
   that you are interested in
2. fill out the information below
3. send form with payment to: Subtotal _____

Family Literacy Center   Shipping _____
Indiana University
2805 E. 10th St., Suite 150   **Total:** _____
Bloomington, IN 47408-2698

Shipping Charges: 1 bk: $2.00   4-7 bks: $4.00
                        2-3 bks: $3.00   8+ bks: $5.00

Name _____

Address _____

_____ Zip _____

Method of payment: ☐ Check   ☐ Money Order
                      ☐ VISA   ☐ MasterCard

Cardholder _____

Card Number _____

Expiration Date _____

        ☐ Please send me the Family Literacy Center catalog!

Books for Home and School

from Grayson Bernard Publishers

❖ *Grammar Handbook for Home and School*
by Carl B. Smith, Ph.D.

A quick reference with concise explanations of the basics of English grammar and punctuation. The perfect companion to *Intermediate Grammar.*

❖ *Intermediate Grammar: A Student's Resource Book*
by Carl B. Smith, Ph.D.

A student's grammatical lifesaver! Complete explanations and examples, plus a handy punctuation guide.

❖ *Elementary Grammar: A Child's Resource Book*
by Carl B. Smith, Ph.D.

A handy source of answers and explanations for young learners and their parents.

Create a success story with ...

Smart Learning: A Study Skills Guide for Teens by William Christen and Thomas Murphy

Learn to focus study time and energy for fantastic results the whole family will be proud of!

. . . and for parents:

The Successful Learner Series

❖ *The Curious Learner: Help Your Child Develop Academic and Creative Skills* by *Marjorie R. Simic, Melinda McClain, and Michael Shermis*

Parents can help their children become curious, well-rounded learners and see the value in all academic and creative pursuits.

❖ *The Confident Learner: Help Your Child Succeed in School* by *Marjorie R. Simic, Melinda McClain, and Michael Shermis*

An easy-to-read, interesting guide for parents of raising a child who is ready and motivated to learn.

"This is an extremely useful and informative book, written by experienced advocates of parental involvement in education."
— *Library Journal*

❖ *Help Your Child Read and Succeed: A Parents' Guide* by *Carl B. Smith, Ph.D.*

Practical, caring advice with skill-building activities for parents and children from a leading expert in the field.

❖ *Expand Your Child's Vocabulary: A Twelve-Week Plan* by *Carl B. Smith, Ph.D.*

A dozen super strategies for vocabulary growth— because word power is part of success at all stages of life.

Find these valuable resources at your favorite bookstore, or use the order form on the next page to have these books sent directly to you.

Order Information

☎ To order by phone, call toll-free 1-800-925-7853 and use your VISA or MasterCard.

✉ To order books by mail, fill out the form below and sen

Grayson Bernard Publishers
P. O. Box 5247, Dept. C2
Bloomington, IN 47407

Qty.	Title	Author	Unit Cost	Total
	Grammar Handbook	Smith, C.	$ 8.95	
	Intermediate Grammar	Smith, C.	$16.95	
	Elementary Grammar	Smith, C.	$13.95	
	Smart Learning	Christen/ Murphy	$10.95	
	The Curious Learner	Simic, M.	$ 9.95	
	The Confident Learner	Simic, M.	$ 9.95	
	Help Your Child Read and Succeed	Smith, C.	$12.95	
	Expand Your Child's Vocabulary	Smith, C.	$ 7.95	

Shipping & Handling
$3.00 for the first book plus $1.00 for each additional book.

Method of Payment
❑ check ❑ money order
❑ Master Card ❑ Visa

Subtotal	
Shipping & Handling	
IN residents add 5% sales tax	
TOTAL	

Card holder_____

Card no. _____

Expiration date _____

Send books to:
Name _____

Address _____

City_____State _____ Zip _____

Prices subject to change.

Your satisfaction is guaranteed.
Any book may be returned within 60 days for a full refund.

Special Offer!

Write or call now for your free year's subscription to Grayson Bernard Publishers' parent newsletter:

Parent & *Child . . . learning together*

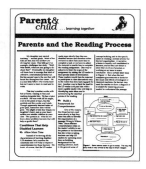

Receive four quarterly issues filled with information and advice all concerned parents need.

Simply mail in the order form below or call (800) 925-7853 for your free subscription.

- -

Name _____

Address _____

City _____ Zip _____

Ages of my children _____

Topics I'd like to read about _____

Mail to: Grayson Bernard Publishers
              Free Subscription Offer
              P.O. Box 5247, Dept. C2
              Bloomington, IN 47407

Grayson Bernard Publishers is a publisher of books for families and educators dedicated to promoting literacy and educational achievement. Our primary goal is to provide quality resources for parents and children to enrich the home learning environment.

For more information about *The Curious Learner* or any of our publications, please contact us at:

Grayson Bernard Publishers
223 S. Pete Ellis Drive, Suite 12
P.O. Box 5247
Bloomington, IN 47407
(800) 925-7853

The **Family Literacy Center** at Indiana University was established to promote family involvement in literacy, which includes all kinds of family activities related to reading, writing, and general communication. The Center engages in research on family literacy, promotes activities and events that encourage family literacy, and sells and disseminates parent involvement materials.

To learn more about the Family Literacy Center, its programs and publications, contact:

Family Literacy Center
Indiana University
2805 E. 10th Street, Suite 150
Bloomington, IN 47408
(800) 759-4723